It is my sincere desire that the owner of this book would find within the pages healing that only comes from our loving and caring Abba-daddy!

I speak a blessing over your life that you will come to know your Abba-daddy in the full measure of his abiding mercy and power that is available to his children.

Sincerely in His Service,

Your Sister and Your Father's Daughter

<u>Mission of the One Heart Series</u>
To provide milk for the babe, and strong meat for the mature. To rid all who come along on this journey of religious traditions that make us white wash graves full of dead men's bones! So, that we may say as the Apostle Paul: "OH" "That I may know him, and the power of his resurrection, and the fellowship of his sufferings, being made conformable unto his death; if by any means I might attain unto the resurrection of the dead. Not as though I had already attained, either were already perfect: but I follow after, if that I may apprehend that for which also I am apprehended of Christ Jesus. Brethren I count not myself to have apprehended: but this one thing I do, forgetting those things which are behind and reaching forth unto those things which are before, I press toward the mark for the prize of the high calling of God in Christ Jesus. Let us therefore, as many as be perfect (pure in heart, italics mine), be thus minded: and if any thing ye be otherwise minded, God shall reveal even this unto you. Nevertheless, whereto we have already attained, let us walk by the same rule, and let us mind the same thing. Brethren, be followers together of me, and mark them which walks so as ye have us for an ensample. (For many walk, of which I have told you often, and now tell you even weeping, that they are the enemies of the cross of Christ: Whose end is destruction, whose God is their belly, and whose glory is their shame, who mind earthly things.) For our conversation is in heaven; from whence also we look for the Saviour, the Lord Jesus Christ; Who shall change our vile body, that it may be fashioned like unto his glorious body, according to the working whereby he is able to even to subdue all things unto himself. (Philippians 3:10-21, KJV)

our vile body, that it may be fashioned like unto his glorious body, according to the working whereby he is able to even to subdue all things unto himself.

Notice is hereby given that this author claims the full trademark rights to the all inferences of the "One", the "Heart", and the name "One Heart Series" utilized throughout the various books, tapes and any and all electronic media used to convey the One Heart Series Message.

© 2003, Patricia E. Adams
™

Copyright © 2003 by Patricia E. Adams

Printed and bound in the United States of America. All rights reserved. No part of this book may be reproduced or transmitted in any form or by any means, electronic or mechanical, including photocopying, recording, or by an information storage and retrieval system -- except by a reviewer who may quote brief passages in a review to be printed in a magazine or newspaper -- without permission in writing from the publisher. For information please contact Shekinah Publishing House, P. O. Box 156423, Fort Worth, Texas 76155, 877/538-1363. Although the author and publisher have made every effort to ensure the accuracy and completeness of information contained in this book, we assume no responsibility for errors, inaccuracies, omissions, or any inconsistency herein. Any slights of people, places, or organizations are unintentional.

Scripture quotations are from the KING JAMES VERSION of the Bible.
Printed in the United States of America

ISBN 0-9700976-3-8
LCCN 99-90788
I and My Father Are One, An Inductive Study of Intimacy with God

---

ATTENTION ORGANIZATIONS, HEALING CENTERS, AND SCHOOLS OF SPIRITUAL DEVELOPMENT:

Quantity discounts are available on bulk purchases of this book for educational purposes. Special books or book excerpts can also be created to fit specific needs. For information, please contact Shekinah Publishing House, P.O. Box 156423, Fort Worth, Texas 76155. 1-877/538-1363.

She is a five-fold minister of the Gospel of Jesus Christ. Licensed in 1993 and Ordained in 1996, and serving her local church of The Potters House of Dallas, Texas. She is a Biblical Studies Instructor at The Potters Institute of Dallas, Texas and an author of a series of books on Inductive Bible Study.

The Series is called "One Heart" and cover how to be intimate with God. There are 5 books in this series. God has placed a strong teaching ministry within her spirit that speaks the truth in love, with a commandment to draw his people out and into an intimate relationship with their God.

God has wrought a mighty deliverance in her life from the baggage of physical, sexual, emotional, and religious bondage. Her testimony is that God is a mighty Deliverer and Restorer.

Patricia is available to share her testimony of deliverance and restoration to groups across the country and around the world. Contact her for

- Revival
- Lectures
- Biblical Seminars
- Writing & Publishing Seminars
- Mass Communication Workshops
- Keynote Address
- Family Seminars (Men, Women and Children)
- Ministry of Helps
- Transitional Housing Outreach

One Heart International Ministries
Patricia E. Adams, President & Founder
Website: www.oneheartseries.com
Affiliate Program: www.oneheartseriesaffiliates.com
Radio Network: www.oneheartsoundmedianetwork.com
Email: author@oneheartseries.com

This book is dedicated to My Many Fathers -
John A.
Thyrah A.
Vernon S.
Fred B.
Tim "Pa-Pa" M.
Phillip B.
God

This dedication is the most complicated of all, because a few on the list existed physically but not emotionally. While others were like having a chaperone and others like a cool drink on a sweltering day! Ultimately, I too must confess that all along my "Father" and "Daddy" has been God! He is listed last not out or disrespect but as the conclusion of the matter. "Special Father" honor goes to Tim "Pa-Pa" M. because of the openness of his heart to take me and mine out of the bulrushes of the Nile as we were adrift leaves me speechless, don't think because the words are few this is an indicator of my love for him. No! It is so much deeper than that, you are missed! Through the love shared by him and his family we are forever grateful! The "Father in the Gospel" honor goes to Phillip B. and I thank him for obeying God when he delivered this message in the pulpit "Choose You this Day," from that day my backsliding was healed as that message came through his mouth from Gods' heart as a confirming word in my life! Through the love shared by him and his family we are forever grateful! Of my fathers it has taken all of them to show me that my true father ultimately was God from beginning to now! Honorable mentions to all mentioned for various conversations and encouraging words. I am truly blessed and to be envied that God again would bless me with so many fathers, as they too have influenced my life! Not all of them have been kind, but God! Again, I won't say which ones, because what the enemy meant for evil God took it and turned it into my good!

ACKNOWLEDGMENTS

First and foremost I thank my "Lord and Savior" for the life experiences and revelation of the truth of His word concerning the trials that have tried me in the fire, and to the enemies of the light of the gospel of Jesus Christ! It is because of these fiery trials and those enemies that this work was accomplished.

To my son, without your understanding and support this work would not have been possible. It is a joy and pleasure being your mother. Much loves to you my Precious!

And to God, who for many nights and early mornings called me into His presence and drew Rhema understanding of why so much pain and suffering had entered my life. He laid the solution before me, and asked me to apply it to the bitterness and pain of the aftershock of what had transpired in my life. For this there is no other that can take the place of Jesus Christ the Lover of My Soul!

We also wish to express special gratitude to the students who attended the initial Bible Study Training. Thank you for your faithfulness in drawing the Word of God out of my belly, and producing a river of living water within me. To Pastor Phillip P. Brown, Sr. and his Wife; Associate Pastor Ethel Brown, for their divine patience in allowing us to bring this material forth in a church bible study for 4 years.

A special appreciation to Pa-Pa and Mother Dear and Aunt Merlee for being there when needed the most. To Momma Tommie, Aunt Margie, Michele, Margie, and Junliah for coming alongside in their diverse ways.

[1] It is not a typographical error. My first mother's last name began with an "M." and the last one mentioned her name too began with an "M."

Introduction

Foundation Scripture:

"And the very God of peace sanctify you wholly; and I pray God your whole spirit and soul and body be preserved blameless unto the coming of our Lord Jesus Christ. Faithful is he that calleth you, who also will do it."

(I Thessalonians 5:23)

Now unto him that is able to keep you from falling, and to present you faultless before the presence of his glory with exceeding joy. To the only wise God our Saviour, be glory and majesty, dominion and power, both now and ever. Amen.

"What is man that though art mindful of him; the Bible records. Man is a tripartite being created in the image of God as an expression of God. The divine plan of God for his created man was that he would love Him with all of himself. This created being would have an absolute desire to fellowship with his creator; from an undivided heart.

Man was created to fulfill the purpose of God in the earth; that is to commune and glory in the benefits of God. The Word of God was the creative force that formed the heavens and the earth, and he alone holds the patent on his creation and the keys to the kingdom. Through the disobedience of one man, Adam; Satan gained legal access, permission to become the Prince of the Air, but not the Ruler of all the earth.

The Bible says that the earth is the Lords and the fullness thereof, and those that dwell within. Ownership has been Gods all alone!

A song was written that said "...What Satan said was his, has been ours all alone..."

Now, Saints Jesus Christ has completed the work that his father sent him to do, and nothing else is required or shall be done. It is finished! Therefore, we should not allow Satan to continue to deceive ourselves into giving away our authority.

If you do not give him access, he can not come in!

Jesus removed Satan's rights to entangle all areas of our lives through the plan of salvation, He restored us to our original posture in God. Yet, we perish because of a lack of knowledge of the provisions of salvation. Especially, when we protect the painful wounds and fearful memories of our lives from God's healing touch. We literally allow a legal playground to be built, played on, and ruled over by Satan and his imps.

When we receive the Holy Spirit into our hearts, he brings in the entire five-fold ministry tools to run a revival in our dead spirit. The Holy Spirit empowers us to operate as God had originally planned. He lifts us from the ashes of despair!

Ashes are used to speak figuratively in the Bible to express the total destruction of a captive city. Ashes are known to be easily scattered, perishable, and, therefore, worthless. For example, when Satan held us as sinners; we were his captive cities.

But when the Power of the Word, the Blood of Jesus and the Fire of the Holy Spirit destroyed, and stripped bare the stronghold, the threat, the penalty and the sting of sin – we were made free! When something is made it is customized to fit the owner. Those strongholds can no longer rule over us, unless we allow them to!

From that landmark of despair, God becomes our Master (Adonai), Owner and Lord. Symbolizing the authority of God and the covenant relationship from the beginning of creation until the ascension of Jesus Christ. Picture an organizational chart, and the Trinity is aligned across the Top; and in a connecting line the second row links and aligns with the first row. This is what the Trinity has done; it has included those who believe with the authority to sit in heavenly places. We are heirs, co-equals with the inheritance of Jesus. Remember the Bible records that, "The Lord said unto my Lord, "Sit thou at my right hand, until I make thine enemies thy footstool." (Psalms 110:1)

In Malachi 4:3, it says that to the Righteous, the wicked deeds of Satan are the "...ashes under the soles of our feet." Not that we are anything in ourselves, but Christ within us is our all. Jesus Christ, the Hope of Glory, Gods' Son and His Anointing took on himself our infirmities, and bore our sicknesses.

If you can envision the Lamb of God as He went to Calvary! Carrying the weight and burden of mans' sinful FLESH, the stinch of disease and the full penalty of sin and it's consequences. There on the cross God laid upon Him the iniquities, and the wages of sin that had separated and broken our fellowship with God. Now as the children of God we partake of that sacrificial lamb, Jesus Christ. Jesus said that he would not drink again, of the cup; or eat of this bread of remembrance until he ascended into heaven.

      He has ascended and destroyed the wage of sin, which was death! Hebrews 2:14, states that Satan's stronghold was destroyed and those who had been held in hell through fear of death who were all their lifetime subject to bondage were released. Through Jesus' death, burial, resurrection and ascension there is deliverance for us today! We have now been settled and grounded in Jesus Christ and His Anointing. As we are continuously filled with the Holy Spirit, enabled or rather empowered to remain steadfast and unmovable, like trees that are planted by the rivers of living water.

Reflection

"Just because someone did not or does not love you the way that you think they should, doesn't mean they don't love you with all they have."

We all know someone, or have known someone or persons who have not loved us as we hoped they would. Whether they were biological, or intimate, or you were victimized by both. They only gave you what they had, but now it is time to move past what they did not have to give us and give ourselves what we deserve! Freedom from carrying around the dead weight of the people who have left us feeling empty and neglected and move into position to receive love from one who can love us to the maximum capacity of what we have made room to receive. Spring (deliverance) is in the air friends, in the natural and the spirit, while we spring clean our houses, garages and offices, how about the clutter in our souls. Just by faith, not by feeling release those who have hurt you in the past and the present from a debt they can not pay, the check you are waiting to cash will bounce anyway, because remember they can not give you what they don't have. Be free in the matchless and marvelous name of the lover of your soul Jesus Christ!" Again, may you find restoration and wholeness on every page for your life!

Your Sister in His Service Until He Shouts!

Objective In: I and My Father Are One

- To move past the baggage of earthly fatherhood that prevents us from embracing the heavenly fatherhood of God
- To receive the blessings of being children of God that will remove the curses of earthly fatherhood
- To receive validation and valuation from the heart of God through his word for his children.
- To receive the purity of the Spirit of Adoption that flows from a Father who chose us! He sent his only begotten son to secure our birthright and adoption into the family of God as his beloved children.
- To open the hearts of earthly fathers towards their children with the pureness of God's love.
- To break the back of and perpetuation of fatherless men and women in our society.
- To provide healing to those who have suffered from the damage of emotional and physical absence, reluctant and perpetual abandonment.

Again, may you find restoration and wholeness on every page of this book for your life!

Table of Contents

ACKNOWLEDGMENTS ix
Introduction x
Reflection xiv
Objective In: I and My Father Are One xv
1-Buried Alive 3
    His Word over My Life 8
    A Kept Woman 14
    Scattered but Not Forgotten 19
    Restoration Gained 20
    Break 25
    Broken For You 26
    But God 40
    Ichabod 48
    Ascension Requires Submission 51
    Ephesians 2:14-18 52
    John 1:1-4, 12-14 52
    Hebrews 12:5-29 53
    Galatians 4:1-11 56
    Romans 10:3 57
    James 4:1-10 58
2- Our Lives before the Cross 67
    Sins of the Eye 80
    Sins of Divination and False Worship 81
    Sins of Anger 81
    Sins of Gluttony 82
    Components of Sin 82
    Lest Ye Be Like the Fig Tree 88
    Stages of the Fig Trees Life 88
    Barren Fig Tree and the Believer 91
    Components of Salvation One(ness) 95
    Reconciliation 98
    Our Lives after the Cross 99
3- The Beatitudes (Blessed Behavior) 105
    Your Behavior Is Telling On You 105
    Beatified 106
    The Nine-Fold Fruits of the Spirit 107

On Christ the Solid Rock We Stand	113
Let Your Glory Fill This Place	119
4- Love	**123**
Love Never Fails	124
GRACE the Number 5	126
He Gave Gifts unto Men	127
Mercy	128
5- After Doing All	**131**
Stand	141
But	142
Scriptural References for What He Will Do When We Stand!	145
How Does He Love Us?	146
6 – The Robe of Many Colors	**153**
The Relationship (Elohim)	153
7 – From Glory to Glory	**157**
Levels of the Relationship	157
The Outer Court Relationship	157
The Inner Court Relationship	159
Brazen Altar	159
Laver	160
Thirsting of Our Souls	161
The Holy Place	161
Holy of Holies	162
The Unlimited Presence	162
The Veil of the Tabernacle	163
Ark of the Covenant	164
The Ten Commandments	164
For All Times	165
What Is In the Name of Jesus' Lineage	168
Reconciling Man to God	173
8 – Abide	**177**
The Fear of the Lord	179
Reverence of God	180
Authority and Fatherhood	181
Sonship and Obedience	182
9 – The Fragrance of the Relationship	**189**
Flies in the Ointments Ecclesiastes 10:1	191
Pre-Extrication	192
A Time of Death and Bondage	192
Sins of Lust	192
Sins of Divination and False Worship	193
Sins of Anger	193
Sins of the Stomach	194
The Prodigal Son and the Older Brother	194
Post-extrication	195

In the Care of God	198
The Zoe	199
Endnotes	201
Other Volumes in the One Heart Series	202

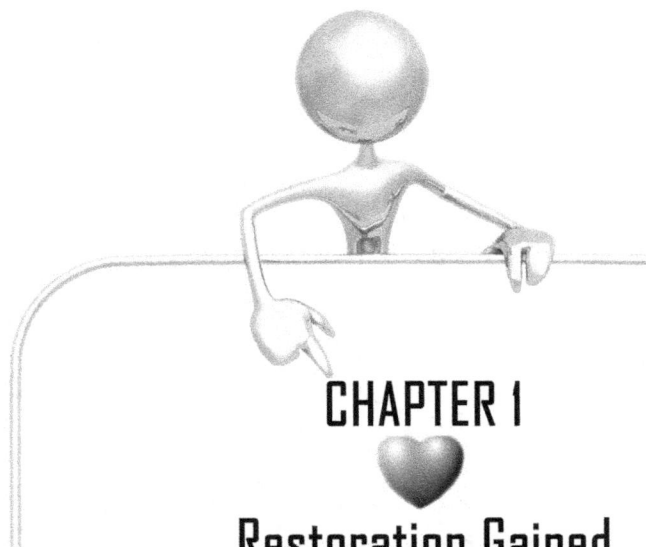

CHAPTER 1

Restoration Gained

"In whatever you do,
strive to do it so well that no man living,
and no man dead and no man yet to be born can do it better."
Benjamin E. Mays

Buried Alive

1-Buried Alive

A voice of a young man called out to me in the distance as I was walking in the botanical gardens. I love walking in the gardens because of the smell and the sights. The green grass and the new life blossoming on stately stems of green; painted against the baby blue horizon of a midday spring sky. How fresh it all makes me feel, but this voice kept calling out to me from the distance; breaking into this serenity that I had found. Turning in the direction of the voice the words were faint but the closer I came to the voice it became clearer. So clear that the words begin to manifest and the words were "Help Me!" It was as if he knew I was passing by or maybe not? Looking for the body to go with the voice and the cry for help frantically now, because the sounds of "Help Me" were getting louder! I felt compelled not to say a word to keep from drowning out his cries. Just as I came to where it seemed the voice was coming from, it stopped suddenly! Oh no I said inside of myself, don't stop now I am here; softly I asked him where he was! He said down here, and my eyes turned downward and yet saw nothing but the plush grass beneath my feet!

Quickly, where are you I asked? He responded - down here! By this time my patience was on the brink of collapse as I still saw no visible sign of anyone being beneath my feet. The ground I stood on was smooth and clean and undisturbed from all appearances. Again he began to say those words frantically "Help Me"!

I dropped to my knees and placed my ear against the ground and called back to him and listened for a response! The sound was echoing up from beneath the very ground I had knelt down on and it frightened me badly. Rising to my feet and jumping off the place where I had knelt to further examine the spot. He begin to say I can hear you and feel the pressure of you standing on the ground above and it is making it hard for me to breathe! Suddenly, it was clear to me that he had been beneath the ground for days and needed help! How could I help him, should I run for help; but first let me mark the spot were I thought he was buried!

He said don't leave me, and I told him that I would be back and he said that someone else told him the same thing two days ago and never came back. He said again "Help Me" "Help Me, Now!" I had no tools to dig with but my hands, kneeling again I began to dig with my hands and my nails hoping he would not give up hope. And hoping someone else would pass by to help me dig or go for help while I kept him assured he would be rescued!

Amazingly he was about 3 feet beneath the surface and as I scratched through the moist soil after breaking the surface of the grass, his right hand popped up and grabbed my hand! Oh my God, did that startle me! A hand reaching from beneath the moist earth clinging to mine for dear life. Thoughts ran through my head - what if he is dangerous or what if this is somebodys idea of a cruel hoax! Surely not, but how did he get there -- no time to ask those questions! We were almost to the point where he could begin helping me free him and then he sneezed as we moved the dirt from his face! He began to panic because he could not see, I told him to calm down because there was still dirt on his face and as soon as we remove the dirt he would be able to see! We moved the dirt from his face and his ears and his eyes and his mouth and he still could not see! He began to panic again and thought he had lost his sight from being beneath the earth and people walking on top of him must have placed pressure on his eyes!

No time I said to him to figure it out because we had to free the rest of him from this place he was buried. He dug with the strength he had and finally he could feel his legs move around. Reaching for his other hand to pull him up with we both struggled and finally he was freed from this place of darkness! He looked at me and I could scarcely make him out beneath the mud on his body. He looked at me and said thank you! As I tried to clean his face some more, this young male voice was an adolescent child peering out from behind that dirt! Before moving him anymore I asked where he was hurting and if he could walk. He said he was very much in pain from being in that space and that before that he had been beaten badly and believed to be dead! Those who had done this buried him thinking he was dead, because the last thing during the beating he remembered was losing consciousness. He had no idea of the time he had spent buried or the day it was, and wanted to be taken to safety! He told me that the people who had done this to him will not be happy to know he was not dead! How could I hide an adolescent boy without involving the authorities. Maybe he is injured internally, maybe he has irreparable harm psychologically and not to mention physical impairments that may arise! What am I suppose to do with this child that was believed dead and is now alive? This day that I walked into the Botanical Gardens to enjoy the beauty of the surroundings had turned into a day of redemption for a young child who thought no one would hear his cries for help! We turn the story to you and ask you today; is that young child you? Are you buried and crying for help and no one seems to hear your cries? Do you think that those who harmed you will stop at nothing to make sure you are dead? What if they find out that you were stronger than they expected and survived the beating and the burial? Could it be that today is the day you get up from the place where they buried you thinking that your story was over? How do you recover when you have been buried alive? My fellow grave partner, the answer is a relationship with Jesus Christ that goes beyond mere words of acceptiing salvation! This gift of salvation is freely yours, but it is the relationship that requires getting to know the one who has saved you and discovering that he has a plan for your lifes' story that exceeds your pain! I invite you to the world of one who was left for dead and buried alive! I am Patricia E Adams, Author of the One Heart Series an Inductive Study on Intimacy with God. This is how the lover of my soul taught me how to overcome the deadly blows that assaulted my body, my spirit, my mind, my soul, my will and my emotions so thoroughly that there should have only been ashes left! But God! He sent His Word and Angels to assure me and rescue me when I was buried alive!

His Word over My Life

At the age of 9 God visited me in a dream or vision I have been told by those more seasoned in the interpretation of dreams. The dream unfolds with mounds of garbage at my feet that it at the ankle left; and garbage is falling down from above onto the ground around me until I am completely covered and buried alive while standing on my feet! Just as suddenly as the breath began to leave my body a bright ray of light broke out from the inside of the garbage heap at my face level! As the light shined into that space a pair of wings flew out from the inside and turned around to face me as I stood still surrounded by the garbage. The wings were holding the letters "Heb. 1:3" between them just like this graphic below reflects before my face!

Hebrews 1:3
1 God, who at sundry times and in divers manners spake in time past unto the fathers by the prophets, 2 Hath in these last days spoken unto us by his Son, whom he hath appointed heir of all things, by whom also he made the worlds; 3 Who being the brightness of his glory, and the express image of his person, and upholding all things by the word of his power, when he had by himself purged our sins, sat down on the right hand of the Majesty on high;

The following morning I went to my adopted mother and told her about the dream and asked her to explain. She asked me to get the Bible and read the scripture to her and I did. She did not have the answer for me and as I look back God hid it from her understanding. Today, I am grateful she did not have the interpretation. Because the things in that dream were an assurance to my nine year old heart that no matter what happened he would see me through. Wonder what would have happened had she known that God had made a way of escape for me? The things he had shown me that night were really about how my life would be as a part of her family. The abuse heaped on me from 7 years until 18 to the near point of death at times suffered at her hands and the hands of her family were detrimental to my spirit! But again GOD!

I Thessalonians 5:23-24

23 And the very God of peace sanctify you wholly; and I pray God your whole spirit and soul and body be preserved blameless unto the coming of our Lord Jesus Christ. 24 Faithful is he that calleth you, who also will do it.

On my own at 18 and the destruction continued until my life seemed would disintegrate into ashes until the age of 24. When he reminded me of the word He had given me at age 9 to keep me from throwing in the towel! By the age of 25 my direction and determination had changed! My expectations for more in my life grew inside of me and I knew no more self-destruction and no more giving away my power! I surrendered to Him conditionally, if you get me out I will never do this or do that or allow this or allow that to happen in my life again! He sent Angels to my RESCUE!

Hebrews 1:4-14

4 Being made so much better than the angels, as he hath by inheritance obtained a more excellent name than they. 5 For unto which of the angels said he at any time, Thou art my Son, this day have I begotten thee? And again, I will be to him a Father, and he shall be to me a Son? 6 And again, when he bringeth in the first begotten into the world, he saith, And let all the angels of God worship him. 7 And of the angels he saith, Who maketh his angels spirits, and his ministers a flame of fire. 8 But unto the Son he saith, Thy throne, O God, is for ever and ever: a sceptre of righteousness is the sceptre of thy kingdom. 9 Thou hast loved righteousness, and hated iniquity; therefore God, even thy God, hath anointed thee with the oil of gladness above thy fellows. 10 And, Thou, Lord, in the beginning hast laid the foundation of the earth; and the heavens are the works of thine hands: 11 They shall perish; but thou remainest; and they all shall wax old as doth

a garment; 12 And as a vesture shalt thou fold them up, and they shall be changed: but thou art the same, and thy years shall not fail. 13 But to which of the angels said he at any time, Sit on my right hand, until I make thine enemies thy footstool? 14 Are they not all ministering spirits, sent forth to minister for them who shall be heirs of salvation?

From that point forward I served him with fervor and gladness until my focus was consumed in religion and doctrines of man! He was gracious to me and had mercy on me as I walked away from the church but not Him. I knew too much about Him and I knew He was real. But could not yet separate Him from Religion. He winked for 13 months at my backslidden condition and finally he had enough and HE CONFRONTED ME! He tore the roof back off of my bedroom ceiling and I looked up at him from my bed of defilement only to be asked "Is that how you want me to find you when I return?" He said to me "Choose you this day whom you will serve." With fear and trembling my soul knew that life and death were before me! What would I do without his grace and mercy over my life? He told me "I would die"! That is when I knew Him as Jehovah Shammah, the One Who Is THERE! And the Omniscient One, the One Who SEES! This is when I was naked and ashamed before Him and the awareness that nothing was hidden from him just because there were walls and ceilings!

Joshua 24:15-17
[15] And if it seem evil unto you to serve the LORD, choose you this day whom ye will serve; whether the gods which your fathers served that *were* on the other side of the flood, or the gods of the Amorites, in whose land ye dwell: but as for me and my house, we will serve the LORD. [16] And the people answered and said, God forbid that we should forsake the LORD, to serve other gods; [17] For the LORD our God, he *it is* that brought us up and our fathers out of the land of Egypt, from the house of bondage, and which did those great signs in our sight, and preserved us in all the way wherein we went, and among all the people through whom we passed:

> He gave me Psalms 51 to use as my daily prayer, sometimes my seconds prayer literally until the process of sanctification had been so thoroughly performed in my life that my backslidings were healed. That was on a Friday and that following Sunday I returned to the household of faith and have remained!

Psalms 51
[1] Have mercy upon me, O God, according to thy loving kindness: according unto the multitude of thy tender mercies blot out my transgressions. [2] Wash me throughly from mine iniquity, and cleanse me from my sin. [3] For I acknowledge my transgressions: and my sin *is* ever before me. [4] Against thee, thee only, have I sinned, and done *this* evil in thy sight: that thou mightest be justified when thou speakest, *and* be clear when thou judgest. [5] Behold, I was shapen in iniquity; and in sin did my mother conceive me. [6] Behold, thou desirest truth in

the inward parts: and in the hidden *part* thou shalt make me to know wisdom. ⁷ Purge me with hyssop, and I shall be clean: wash me, and I shall be whiter than snow. ⁸ Make me to hear joy and gladness; *that* the bones *which* thou hast broken may rejoice. ⁹ Hide thy face from my sins, and blot out all mine iniquities. ¹⁰ Create in me a clean heart, O God; and renew a right spirit within me. ¹¹ Cast me not away from thy presence; and take not thy holy spirit from me. ¹² Restore unto me the joy of thy salvation; and uphold me *with thy* free spirit. ¹³ *Then* will I teach transgressors thy ways; and sinners shall be converted unto thee. ¹⁴ Deliver me from blood guiltiness, O God, thou God of my salvation: *and* my tongue shall sing aloud of thy righteousness. ¹⁵ O Lord, open thou my lips; and my mouth shall shew forth thy praise. ¹⁶ For thou desirest not sacrifice; else would I give *it*: thou delightest not in burnt offering. ¹⁷ The sacrifices of God *are* a broken spirit: a broken and a contrite heart, O God, thou wilt not despise. ¹⁸ Do good in thy good pleasure unto Zion: build thou the walls of Jerusalem. ¹⁹ Then shalt thou be pleased with the sacrifices of righteousness, with burnt offering and whole burnt offering: then shall they offer bullocks upon thine altar.

From here he asked if I wanted to be kept? I said emphatically "Yes" knowing that without His keeping POWER I would surely fail! From that moment until now I have been His KEPT Woman! Nobody can keep you like He can!

A Kept Woman

Jude 1:15-25

15 To execute judgment upon all, and to convince all that are ungodly among them of all their ungodly deeds which they have ungodly committed, and of all their hard speeches which ungodly sinners have spoken against him. 16 These are murmurers, complainers, walking after their own lusts; and their mouth speaketh great swelling words, having men's persons in admiration because of advantage. 17 But, beloved, remember ye the words which were spoken before of the apostles of our Lord Jesus Christ; 18 How that they told you there should be mockers in the last time, who should walk after their own ungodly lusts. 19 These be they who separate themselves, sensual, having not the Spirit. 20 But ye, beloved, building up yourselves on your most holy faith, praying in the Holy Ghost, 21 Keep yourselves in the love of God, looking for the mercy of our Lord Jesus Christ unto eternal life. 22 And of some have compassion, making a difference: 23 And others save with fear, pulling them out of the fire; hating even the garment spotted by the flesh. 24 Now unto him that is able to keep you from falling, and to present you faultless before the presence of his glory with exceeding joy, 25 To the only wise God our Saviour, be glory and majesty, dominion and power, both now and ever. Amen.

This scripture too became my accompanying prayer to Psalms 51 and between those two they were like a one-two punch to the vain imaginations that flooded my memory bank! When something would replay in my life these two would be applied with fervor instantly and repeatedly until my mind was renewed. Then he told me to change my thoughts from that point on to maintain my deliverance through submitting my thought life to the power of transformation!

Philippians 4:8
Finally, brethren, whatsoever things are true, whatsoever things are honest, whatsoever things are just, whatsoever things are pure, whatsoever things are lovely, whatsoever things are of good report; if there be any virtue, and if there be any praise, think on these things.

I had a poster that would be on my wall in the bathroom as I would get ready for my day, in my bedroom and by my computer until I would rehearse this in my mind at the first glance of drifting thoughts! And Jude 1:15-25 became the partner to Philippians 4:8 to maintain my thought life! I had given Him control over my life from the physical to the spiritual! I wanted to be kept wholly His! No more cheating on Him and no more backsliding as he promised he would in ...

Jeremiah 3:22 22
Return, ye backsliding children, and I will heal your backslidings. Behold, we come unto thee; for thou art the LORD our God.

From that Friday night when the roof came off until this day "our relationship" has gotten sweeter and sweeter as the days go by! He has become my husband! This is what I believe God desires we allow him to become to us our first love! To the woman her husband and to the man his wife! You may struggle with that, but remember God is a Spirit and not confined to gender biases. He is the " I Am that I Am"! What affect would this have on the divorce rate?

Song of Songs 2:4

4 He brought me to the banqueting house, and his banner over me was love.

I invite you to continue through on this journey of intimacy with God or to get started because He longs for you more than you long for Him! For those of you who have been on this journey through the One Heart Series it has been the process of working out your soul salvation so you would be able to stand ready when the Bridegroom cometh! Light has shined into the darkness of what the enemy meant for evil and has been comprehended! He has so thoroughly completed every promise that I have received and believed into my life! Those promises that He has made you are worth more than gold and totally obtainable and non-expiring!

Song of Songs 3:4

4 It was but a little that I passed from them, but I found him whom my soul loveth: I held him, and would not let him go, until I had brought him into my mother's house, and into the chamber of her that conceived me.

This journey started in 1989, on that Friday where God asked her to draw closer to Him, and he would reveal my place of healing would be in the unity of our time of intimacy. He birthed the One Heart Series out of our relationship. Because of this the journey starts at the present state of the heart in the absence of the transforming power of Salvation. That state is one of shame, self-hatred and God-hatred and unpeels the shame, self-hatred and superficiality that prevents us from loving God with our whole heart. Which compels us to remove the layers of fig leaves we often hide behind in the Outer Court Relationship and become naked before God in the Inner Court Relationship of Spiritual Intimacy with God as our Lover, Lord and King of Glory. You are encouraged as a believer to become transparent before God by stripping away the superficiality of our souls and bare all in the presence of God. By embracing the pureness of God's love for us and enter into the process of sanctification. The toxic seeds that ravage our emotions, imprison us to the past, torment our present and sabotage our future are confronted and quality decisions are made to break up the crop and replant seeds of righteousness. We then begin the journey of progression and cancel the round trips of regression into the video vault of the past. Coming out of the wilderness of victimization and firmly planted onto the road of victor, because we recognize we are created for purpose and that purpose is great! We are healed of our backslidings by exploring the issues of the unsurrendered heart going through the process of Salvations transformation. And it is in this volume we validate the surrendered heart as His Beloved and that surrendered heart is Safe in Gods vast arms. We are abiding in the secret place of the Most High in the Inner Court relationship. Salvation has had its perfect work inside and we live as we are lived in. Reproach of shame, self-hatred and God-hatred has been rolled away and we are in love and love is in our whole heart. Clothed in righteousness and still naked because the layers of fig leaves are removed allowing us to rest, recline and bask in our spiritual intimacy with God as our Lover, Lord, King of Glory and Father. Now let us look at the restoration God has provided for us through the sacrificial offering of His Son Jesus Christ!

John 1:3-4 says that "What we have seen and heard we also declare to you, so that you may have fellowship along with us; and indeed our fellowship is with the Father and with His Son Jesus Christ. We are writing these things so that our joy may be complete"

Because of the experience I have had in my life with God through His First Begotten Son, "Jesus Christ" I am compelled to share our relationship with you and the testimony of his love towards me! It is with this great joy that this journey of pure intimacy is shared through my heart from Gods' heart of love!

Zechariah Chapter 2 speaks of the consequences of rebelling against God! He intends to repair even that which has been scattered, because he loves too vastly to ever give up eternally on his people!

2:1 I lifted up mine eyes again, and looked, and behold a man with a measuring line in his hand. 2 Then said I, Whither goest thou? And he said unto me, To measure Jerusalem, to see what is the breadth thereof, and what is the length thereof. 3 And, behold, the angel that talked with me went forth, and another angel went out to meet him, 4 And said unto him, Run, speak to this young man, saying, Jerusalem shall be inhabited as towns without walls for the multitude of men and cattle therein: 5 For I, saith the LORD, will be unto her a wall of fire round about, and will be the glory in the midst of her. 6 Ho, ho, come forth, and flee from the land of the north, saith the LORD: for I have spread you abroad as the four winds of the heaven, saith the LORD. 7 Deliver thyself, O Zion, that dwellest with the daughter of Babylon. 8 For thus saith the LORD of hosts; After the glory hath he sent me unto the nations which spoiled you: for he that toucheth you toucheth the apple of his eye. 9 For, behold, I will shake mine hand upon them, and they shall be a spoil to their servants: and ye shall know that the LORD of hosts hath sent me. 10 Sing and rejoice, O daughter of Zion: for, lo, I come, and I will dwell in the midst of thee, saith the LORD. 11 And many nations shall be joined to the LORD in that day, and shall be my people: and I will dwell in the midst of thee, and thou shalt know that the LORD of hosts hath sent me unto thee. 12 And the LORD shall inherit Judah his portion in the holy land, and shall choose Jerusalem again. 13 Be silent, O all flesh, before the LORD: for he is raised up out of his holy habitation.

Restoration Gained

God has always had a plan to restore to his people access to His Kingdom. And Satan has always had a plan to keep us from that access. The first Adam lost our legal rights and authority to the Kingdom. The second Adam restored our legal authority and access to the keys of the Kingdom.

It is obvious throughout the Biblical and secular history that awareness has existed in mankind that there is something better than to be had. So we pursue that which we are not sure of when we are in the secular realm. We think the missing link is materialism. Yet the more we get the more we need to keep us feeling complete.

But when we enter into the spiritual realm our focus changes. We no longer seek the things that are temporary and subject to change, but seek the one who is permanent and unchangeable. I will forever see Satan as the original Father of child abuse. He knew that the place of exile for him could not compare to the place and authority he possessed in heaven. Satan lied on his way out of the glory to a third of the host of heaven's angels and deceived them into joining him. Since then that host of reprobates longs for what it cannot have. Thus the war ensues to keep you from what you can have.

It becomes real apparent why misery loves company. Who wants to start a kingdom without somebody to serve him or her. A king without a kingdom is only a figurehead. Satan needed others to help him in his futile pursuit to against God. Truthfully spoken, Satan could care less about us! Satan hates God! And will use any measure to hinder the advancement of God's kingdom. This in itself is unbelievable, because the Bible declares there is no power except that which God delegates. So even the power he has is that which God allowed him to keep in his fallen nature.

God could have destroyed Satan and his band of insurrectionist with one thought. But no, our sovereign and all powerful God, abided by his own law of reciprocity '...that there is a time and a season for all things.' God has set laws in motion to govern the entire universe. Heaven's Accountant is duly noting every transaction that Satan makes, and those who yield their bodies as members/instruments. The unrighteous shall receive their payment in full in due season. The Law of Sowing and Reaping has no respect of person or deed, whether good or evil. The Sower of the seed determines the harvest to be reaped. When this or any of Gods' universal laws are transgressed the penalty is attached to the law and it becomes a part of your genetic makeup spiritually and naturally.

You see for every seed of curses planted an equal number of seeds of blessings are required to be planted to cancel the harvest of curses.

Let's read Luke 22:31,34,40, 61-62: "...and the Lord said, Simon, Simon, behold, Satan hath desired to have you, that he may sift you as wheat: But I have prayed for thee, that thy faith fail not: and when thou are converted strengthen thy brethren. And he said Lord, I am ready to go with thee, both into prison, and to death. And he said, I tell thee, Peter, the cock shall not crow this day, before that thou shalt thrice

(3) deny that thou knowest me. (31,34)...

And when he was at that place, he said unto them, Pray that ye enter not into temptation. (40)...

And the Lord turned, and looked upon Peter. And Peter remembered the word of the Lord, how he had said unto him, Before the cock crow, thou shalt deny me thrice. (62)...

And Peter went out, and wept bitterly.

So when they had dined, Jesus saith to Simon Peter, Simon, son of Jonas, lovest thou me more than these? He saith unto him, yea, Lord; thou knowest that I love thee. He saith unto him feed my lambs. He saith to him again the second time, Simon, son of Jonas, lovest thou me? He saith unto him, the third time, Lovest thou me? And he said unto him Lord thou knowest all things, thou knowest that I love thee. Jesus saith unto him feed my sheep. (John 21)"

Notice three times Peter denied Jesus, and three times Peter had to confess that he did know him to cancel the debt. Remember the saying 'To know him is to love him.' When you love someone, you acknowledge that before anybody at anytime. So, as I come into God's revelation knowledge I alter my spiritual and genetic makeup. I cancel out the seeds of curses and plant seeds of blessing to create the harvest of God's divine plan for my life and my future generations. Even now yokes are being destroyed in my life, and so too in yours. Amen.

We must allow God to mold, break, pluck and plant in me the powerful rhema from His Word, until that harvest is cancelled out of my generational line. We all have this choice, it is found in Deuteronomy 8 and Deuteronomy 28.

All of the stealing, killing and destroying that Satan has done are links in the chain that God will use to bind him with! Halleluia! There is a time reserved for Satan and those who will be found numbered among them. Even those of the Body of Christ Jesus who are deceived will be cut off from the vine and cast into the fire. Don't you be found in that number with the transgressors.

Church Satan has a harvest to reap and it is not worth being a part of that stinking – sulphuric fire hole God has reserved for him. When we yield ourselves to evil we are just pawns and instruments used at all costs in the war Satan wages against God. The unsaved, backslidden or lukewarm are soldiers in the army of the living dead. Satan will use us until he destroys us, or until we get out of his realm of darkness, and walk in the light of our salvation.

For this cause God loved us enough to send his glory through the flesh of one named Jesus. It is the one called

Jesus who rent the veil of his flesh to provide a permanent way of escape from the enemies' concentration camp. It is God in Him, and He in God that gives us the right to the keys of the kingdom. God broke himself for as many of us through an available and obedient vessel so that we might not smell like rotting flesh, but smell of the fragrance of life. He died in our place, so that we might live and live more abundantly.

Break

Let's examine the word break – Broken in heart … (Psalms 109:16). In the Hebrew the word is Kaah.

Al Novak, in his 1965 version of Hebrew Honey, said "To be crushed is another idea brought out in Psalms 10:10. This leads to despondency, which is a fall down toward despair….It means to be frightened or intimidated, "whipped out of the land", (See Job 30:8). This is the principal idea in Kaah.

So, we have the history of many church members: Chided; made sad, broken in heart; grieved; frightened out of God's vineyard. **But We Know The Breaker Who Breaks The Cords Of Satan!**

In 1999 when the church was rejoicing over the natural Jubilee revelation of the 50th year of Israel as a Nation, I rejoiced too, but then I thought wait a minute I don't want to wait for another one to come by before I rejoice in the Jubilee. Then God revealed to me that every second, every minute, every hour, every day, every week, every month, every year is Jubilee. Everything that was required by Law had been presented to the Judge of Heaven and from the point of Salvation I entered Jubilee. But why does it take so long for the manifestation, I asked? And He spoke, you tell me! I was taken back, and I began to think on this – and discovered that I find no fault in Him. He has done all that needs to be done. All of the healing, all of the blessing, all of the wealth giving, all of the peace making, all of the identity changing that needs to be done and will ever be done. God spoke through his Son in the greatest battle day the mind has ever known – and proclaimed it is finished! And now He (Jesus) is seated in a position of rest and reign in high places. And with that revelation I became sorrowful that it had taken so long for me to reach up and out to Him. When I did, God revealed to me that I had accepted his love for me as his bride, and I became a woman who knows she is unconditionally loved! This love Jesus through the Holy Spirit is reflected in my body, physically and spiritually.

That Holy Spirit is none other than Jesus Christ – seated and pouring out his self into the earth and into these earthen vessels. Acts 3:32-35, confirms it. Peter says, "This Jesus God has raised up, of which we are all witnesses. Therefore being exalted to the right hand of God, and having received from the Father the promise of the Holy Spirit, He poured out this, which you now see and hear. For David did not ascend into the heavens, but he says himself: 'The Lord said to my Lord, Sit at My right hand, Till I make Your enemies Your footstool."

Who is Jesus, but God in the Flesh, and if that be so; then that which is being poured out by God is of God and He is that same Jesus pouring out himself.

Through the power of the Holy Spirit many unfulfilled people who have mask themselves in external garments and participate in Mardi Gras and Carnivale can come out and be free to be themselves in the light of day. Because of the rejection many have experienced in their lives from others and themselves, are they dwelling in the dens and hangouts of darkness. Come Forth! Come Forth! Lazarus Come Forth! Into the light of day that is none other than Jesus

Christ, whom all things are laid bare before. The spirit of rejection carries a stench that permeates the entire spirit – I have smelt sour odors when exposed to this spirit. It overflows from their conversation into their everyday lives. Contaminating the air and anything they touch. It is like taking a daily dosage of slow death.

Now, let's examine the composition of the word rejection: The word referenced in Zodhiates Word Study Dictionary, number 96 is A-dokimos.

A- means without; and Dokimos means acceptance.

Literally rendered as one who is unapproved, unworthy, spurious, worthless, and a castaway. In I Corinthians 9:27,

Paul said that his own behavior would cause him to be Adokimos, not subject to Christ. Also in II Corinthians 13:5-7, we are told to examine ourselves, not others to see if we are in the faith. Meaning is the Word of God in us and in control of our spirit. Hebrews 6:8, shows that uncontrolled behavior is full of thorns and briers. The kinds of thorns that would and could hold us in bondage, and ensnare others in the brier patch.

Finally, in I Peter 2:4-7 we are to be full of the life that heals and delivers us first – so that we can deliver others.

Many of us who have been born again for decades are running to every Prophet, and every man, woman, and child that display in their ministry an element of deliverance.

God is the DELIVERER. He is available to all who are nigh to him. Lay hands on yourself! Before anybody can speak deliverance over you they have to deliver themselves or go to somebody else for assistance. I am not knocking deliverance. God has used me in this area, but I have come to see that the answer to the people's problem is almost one inch below their nostril. All they need to do is "Speak the Word ONLY" and it shall be. Develop your intimate relationship with God, and open your mouth and speak to the mountains. How can a prisoner release another prisoner? Until that prisoner has been released or escaped they cannot carry others out. Note, Moses – before he could lead the people out he had to free himself first; from the grips of Pharaoh and Egypt.

Disobedience breeds an environment that produces a path ladened with stumbling blocks. The stones of that path are laid with rocks of offenses given and received.

Thorns and briers grow up between the paths ready to snare us, and cause us to ensnare others. A constant state of confusion and frustration keeps us walking along this path with our vision impaired by a continual fog of nothingness. We stumble alone feeling nothing of the joys of life, and feeling like nothing.

Rehearsing all the lies we have been told and have a life long pity party. Repeating these phrases "they always said I wouldn't be nothing, my momma, my grand momma, my daddy, and my granddaddy weren't nothing'. So we treat our selves and let others treat us like nothing. Exoudenoo means to treat as nothing as in Matthew 21:42-43, the disciple of the Lord says that Jesus told them "Did ye never read the scriptures, the stone which the builders rejected, the same is become the head of the corner: this is the Lord's doing, and it is marvelous in our eyes? Therefore say I unto you, The Kingdom of God shall be taken from you, and given to a nation bringing forth the fruits thereof. And whosoever shall fall on this stone shall be broken: but on whomsoever it shall fall, it will grind him to powder."

Then in Matthew 22:8-14, Jesus continues to say "Then saith he to his servants, the wedding is ready, but they which are bidden were not worthy. Go ye therefore into the highways, and as many as ye shall find, bid to the marriage. So those servants went out into the highways, and gathered together all as many as they found, both bad and good: and the wedding was furnished with guests." Jesus knows what it is like to be treated as nothing. He bore our infirmities (weaknesses) for us. Part of our infirmities was the state of nothingness we were condemned to live in. Satan had a hold on our lives and he treated us as nothings and nobodies. But listen, Jesus is also saying that if once we have been invited to the marriage supper and we refuse to come or to even acknowledge his extended invitation. Then we too are guilty of treating Jesus Christ as nothing.

There is no excuse for this behavior, because with the invitation from Jesus to the guest, came the ability (the grace) to answer. When we accept the invitation of salvation, Jesus is saying that he is well able to provide the necessary provisions we require in this life. But if we reject the invitation, because we are too busy trying to make a way for ourselves in the world we treat him as nothing. God has removed the drudgery out of living for you and I, children of God. He has told us that he is our ever-present help in the time of trouble. He has told us to trust in him with all of our hearts, and lean not to our own understanding, and in all of our ways acknowledges him and he would direct our paths. He has taken us off the street called 'Nowhere', and placed us on the street called 'Somewhere.'

He is the ever present, Jehovah Shammah. He knows what street you were on when you were raped, molested, starving, cold, naked and afraid. The name of the street was 'Nowhere' in the 01 B.C., and it still has the same name today in 1999. God has not forgotten about us, it is us who has forgotten about him.

We must quickly run to the corner of 'Nowhere', where it intersects with 'Somewhere' and cross over to the other side, and demand Satan to back off. He is trespassing when he tries to hang out on our property, stand up and put the devil in his place, and no be whipped out of God's presence.

We have been granted an eternal and irrevocable invitation to be in the presence of the Lord of Host.

Satan would have you believe that you are unworthy. Remember Satan is capable of telling part of the truth, but not the whole truth. You as an unsaved creation cannot be worthy. You (meaning your natural abilities, skills, talents and physical body) could get you into hell, but not into heaven. But you the saved by grace child of God has been made worthy through the righteousness of Jesus. One greater than our selves has destroyed the works of Satan and to gain our liberty. He is the BREAKER of the breaker. When were members of Satan's family we were truly unworthy of God! Let me direct your attention to the prodigal son, which is an example of the liberation that points towards our worthiness.

Luke 15:11, reads "And he said, A certain man had two sons…the younger of them said to his father, Father, give me the portion of goods that falleth to me…not many days…and took his journey into a far country, and there wasted his substance…he had spent all…he began to be in want…when he came to himself…I will arise and go to my father, and will say…Father, I have sinned…and am no more worthy to be called thy son…when he was a great way off, his father saw him, and had compassion, and ran, and fell on his neck and kissed him. And the son said…I have sinned…and am no more worthy to be called thy son. BUT the father said…bring forth the best robe…"

The best robe meant that he did not see the son, as the son saw himself. The son saw himself as unworthy and unfit to be a son. Even though he was willing to be treated as a servant – the son saw himself even lower than that of a servant. But in the eyes of the Father, he never ceased to be his son. But the condition of the relationship was one of distance. Most people will agree it is difficult to maintain an intimate relationship at a distance. Intimacy requires a close encounter. God says in his word that he is married to the backslider! Not the unsaved, but to those who once had entered into his unconditional heart of love. The sons' returning home was an acknowledgement of his backslidden state. It required that he turn from his wicked ways (repent) and come back on the same path he had chosen to leave on. The prodigal son chose to leave the world behind, just as he had chosen earlier to leave the presence of his Father's house. A clear decision was made to stop hanging out on the front porch of the house, and come into the house and act like a son. The symbolism of the Father putting on the best robe, is the equivalent of God our Father, putting his best robe on us 'JESUS', which is nothing else but Jesus' blood and righteousness clothing us today. Which allows God the Father to look at us and not see our past, present or future – because all of these are hidden in Christ Jesus. When God sees us he sees the image of his Son imposed onto our image -- without blemish, conforming us to holiness. It is through the robe of shed blood known as Jesus' that we are worthy.

Now let's look at the word unworthy in the Greek. Remember the letter 'A' means without. The root word genealogetou means genealogy. Put the two together and the word means unworthy. Without genealogy or pedigree like "Melchizedec." He was said to be without pedigree in Psalms 110:4, without genealogy as the other Levitical priest were from Aaron (Exodus 40:15, Number 3:10, & Hebrews 7:3) which proved their right to the priesthood.

This state of being an outsider and nobody has been cast away from us as far as the east is to the west. We were once without parentage, separated at birth by sin. We were bastards and orphans. No more, we are now Sons and Daughters of the King of Heaven, the Most High God!

What was it like to be on the outside and without?

A= without

Metor= record of mother

Pator = record of father. Mark 12:35

The practice of the priesthood being selected from one lineage existed under the Old Testament. Notice I said, under – means we were obligated – weighted down year after year as not being fit to be a High Priest in the House of God. Again, no more this has been done away with according to Hebrews 11:38.

This passage says that we are worthy to be his friends, and to be cherished by him and others. We are free from the curse of the law of sin and death. Through the Prophet

Isaiah's rendering of the death, burial and resurrection of Jesus Christ we are aware that even then 400 years before his manifestation – God has us on his mind.

His body was broken for us as recorded in Romans 5:8. We demonstrate and fulfill his death, shed blood, burial and resurrection every time we worship in communion. We are symbolically drinking the strength of the life contained in the blood of a sinless Jesus Christ. The covenant he made with us that he would never leave us or forsake us being fulfilled.

The Word of God, and scientific evidence indicates that life is in the blood. Through the sprinkling and the application of the blood we wave the banner of victory flying overhead us openly and defiantly.

Proving to us, and drawing the line between Satan, and us that he is a defeated foe. Our sins have been forgiven, and his legal access to our lives has been revoked. We receive the sacrifice of communion with our hands, indicating that we are to accept and digest what has been done for us. The Prophet Jeremiah was told to eat the whole thing, the bitter and the sweet. Digest and comprehend the bitterness of sin, and the sweetness of victory in Christ Jesus.

In response as an act of adoration we are to use these same hands to serve, as Jesus has served us. Our hands are given as instruments of service to one another, to prepare the way, praise him into our presence, and lift up the name of God. Not to gratify the lust of our flesh or each other's flesh.

I would like to interject a revelation that God gave me about our hands serving ourselves. Perhaps you will find it inappropriate at this point in the text, but I think not! When we use our hands to bring sexual gratification we literally take our spirit into the realm of the darkness of immorality. When we have fantasy sex, phone sex our spirits are joined with the other spirit on the other end of the line, and we are participating in a ritual of whoredoms and idolatry. Serving self.

Does God get the glory out of that, no I think not. He gets no glory out of your erotic releases or the releases of others outside or inside of marriage. When we are self-gratifying a state of trance takes over us that entertains the fantasies of the mind. Fantasies about Joe, Danny, Frankie, Jane, Conchita, Lena, – and you know whoever else we have desires for presently -- this week. At that moment of entertainment the spirit is dry, and demons enter where. In dry places! I believe that from a Holy God comes a Holy life. Mind you I did not say bland.

Just read the Song of Solomon to your husband or wife sometimes and see the pureness of romance flourish as God intended. It is with our mouths that we build up, edify and exhort one another in all things. God is excited by our conversation when it is focused on Him!

So, why must we use the things that we used when we were outside of his presence to satisfy us in his presence? I know he has a more excellent way! Maybe you are to ready put this down and turn me off. But, I can afford to be right or wrong, but can you afford to be wrong? Why don't you prove God! Your hands cannot possibly be lifted up as holy and serve and worship the living God while serving your selfish desires. Can you visualize worshipping God and serving yourself with the same hands at the same time? He sees what we do openly and privately. Is He as pleased with your private person as he is with your public person? If He came back while you were getting your groove on would you be embarrassed or proud of how he finds you. If you cringed at the thought of that – then you know that I am speaking the truth to you from God. He confronted me, before I confronted you. Speaking the truth in love is my call!

Put away the deeds of the flesh today!

The Bible says "...let no flesh glory in his presence." Colossians 3:1-3 "If then you be raised with Christ, seek those things which are above, where Christ is, sitting at the right hand of God. Set your mind on things above, not on things on the earth. For you died, and your life is hidden with Christ in God. When Christ who is our life appears, then you also will appear with Him in glory. Therefore put to death your members, which are on the earth: fornication, uncleanness, passion, evil desire and covetousness, which is idolatry. Because of these things the wrath of God is coming upon the sons of disobedience, in which you yourselves once walked when you lived in them."(NKJV)

Maybe you want to pick up your Bible and say, well God said if it offends my brother then don't … but he didn't say don't do it when I am not with my brother. You know how we do – when we want to have our way. Well anyway – I am FREE! So have it your way! Let's go further down the road.

This behavior is not befitting of the bride who is living a life hidden in the groom (Jesus). We are no longer without parentage, but with parentage because of Jesus' perfectly serving the duties of communion as the Paschal Lamb (without blemish), the unleavened (without sin) bread, wine (covenant blood spoken of between God and Abraham), and eating the bitter herb of (death) with an righteous heart in the office of the High Priest. To be without (on the outside looking in) we were bastards, now we are sons, robed and clothed in the righteousness of Jesus. We are worthy saints, to praise God in the sanctuary, not just the place you attend church. But in the sanctuary, which is you. You are free to lift up holy hands! Praise God! Let's behave accordingly little children.

Some of you know what it is like to be without a genealogy. Somebody, somewhere is reading this and have never met their mother or father. They don't even know who they are. Well, I can identify I been there done that for a season, before I found mine. But God has given me the victory, and a parentage that is royal, holy and altogether lovely. Through the Spirit of Adoption, whereby (I) we cry out Abba, My dear Daddy! I love you!

But God
___

Has given to us without ametros (measure). We should never boast of ourselves and condemn what others are not doing. When the work at hand is immeasurable. What we have done is not even a fraction of an inch in the measure of what Jesus did, and continues to do. (II Corinthians 11:5, II Corinthians 12:11.)

A picture of Jesus is seen through the recording of the High Priest - Melchizedek. Jesus made us to become sons of God by performing the duties of the High Priest without interruption (24x7), and we are no longer bastards (24x7). He had no need of dependence on human genealogies as recorded throughout history. It was not about who your parents were or weren't. It was about who the Alpha and Omega IS!

He said, "I am that I am" ... there is none like Him on the earth or under the earth. He has reconciled the chasm that separated us from His creation and to boot gave us a promotion to the position of Sonship. He defeated the physical through the spiritual, and drew a line that reaches from his heavenly father (who was masculine enough to be Daddy and gentle enough to be Mommy -- all by His great awesome self. He was meek enough to become a little child and attach himself to a natural woman's uterus and incubate for nine months. Then come forth with the breaking of the woman's water (to inform us that it is not by power, nor by might, but by his Spirit being poured out). He was the word being made flesh. His flesh was pressed out as the olives are pressed out to draw out the oil. So this pressing brought out the character of God in himself. Because of this character he was able to bear the burden of the cross. What he was in life he was in death. Only because of his lifestyle could he have died as God. He lived the life he talked about. He was training for the Olympics of the Cross all of his 30 plus years, for that one main event. They say what is in you will come out when under pressure. All of God was in him, and Satan found nothing of himself in Jesus. That is why Jesus was able to tell Satan "You CAN'T Touch." People can identify you with your children because they have something of you in them. So ought folk be able to identify you with your daddy GOD! Jesus identified with his Father and not the condemned Satan. Jesus has poured out himself as the water is poured forth from a woman's womb at the entrance of a new life. None other than the Holy Spirit, he has given us himself as a friend (the Holy Spirit). When the spirit leaves a body it is no longer present in the earth. But when Jesus commended his spirit to God. He did so with the purpose of pouring it out into the earthen vessels that would receive it with an open mouth (heart). You can't pour anything into a closed jar. But a wide mouth jar can take as much as it is suited to contain.

Have you opened your heart and allowed him to come in and sup with you?

Jesus has ratified the old covenant and fulfilled it to the letter, signed it, sealed it in the blood of him, and set himself down next to himself and cried Abba Father. Placed his legs up on his footstool (Satan). He has become our counselor (lawyer) and our executor of our estate. He continues to disburse the inheritance of the saints to those who are willing and obedient to eat the good of the land. Somebody shout Halleluia!!!!

He took the only legal key that Satan had to dominate -- fallen man away from Satan. Then whipped him for his effort in Hell, and declared that he had risen with all power in his hands. O death where is thy sting, o grave where is thy victory -- it has been swallowed up!

You ought to be getting undressed and throwing away those old grave clothes by now and determining to put on your new clothes and preparing yourself to be his bride right now! Repent and confess your sins to God and be made whole in the name of Jesus. Amen. The question is "Wilt thou be made whole?"

God used Satan's (the Prosecutions) legal key witness; fallen man was represented by Joseph as a proxy of the original fallen man, in the book of Matthew. Joseph testified, "This was not wrought of my flesh, but of the Spirit of God." Then God called Gabriel to support his claim! Then the star witness Eve, who was represented in Mary – was called to testify about how Satan was a liar from the beginning, and a deceiver too.

God then delivered his final deliberation before the Jury of Heaven. Satan thought that he would use the story of Job to write the conclusion to what I planned for my people before the foundation of the earth. I told Satan then that he could try Job, but he could not kill him. I knew that even though Job felt like I had slain him and destroyed him – yet I knew that he would not curse me and die. If he had cursed me he would surely have died. So today I call all of the Hall of Faith witnesses to testify against the prosecutions claim that all of my creation would reject me and die.

God then compels the witnesses in the earth to take record of the witnesses in heaven, and see that it is finished. When Joseph and Mary, chose to obey God rather than Satan their eyes were opened. Unlike the fallen man and woman of old. Satan had no choice but, to surrender and declare that he could no longer perjure himself against the truth. Yes, you are God all by yourself. The defenses closing remarks were "It is finished."

The death penalty was carried out on Golgotha (the place of the mind), and with the burial of the body, all debts were cancelled against those who would believe on him. For God so loved the world that he gave his only begotten son. Heaven and earth witnessed the great escape! God pronounced with a loud voice through his son's Jesus vocal cords "LET MY PEOPLE GO." Those are they whose robes have been washed in the blood of the lamb. They were allowed to go free and to be reinstated without delay to their position of royalty in the kings' palace. From the legal line of Adam, and the covenant line of Abraham, picked up the royalty promised to Abraham through David, and the physical suit of separation from Joseph and Mary.

Reconciled them, removed the wall of separation by race, gender and parentage-- made them one. Jeremiah says, to paraphrase 'he made it again another' and the records of creation says, 'in the beginning the word was God, and the word was with God, and without God was nothing made that was made.'

Through this entire lineage there existed no priestly ancestry in the tribe of Judah, but He (Jesus) was of the tribe of Judah and not the tribe of Levi (Aaronical Priesthood).

Proving that race was no longer an issue. He was going to use the race of mankind to win the world for his kingdom. It takes all of us to be ready for the bridegrooms return. As Melchizedek's prototype, Christ the King became Christ our High Priest who stood alone and unique in His priesthood and is absolutely distinct from the long succession of Aaronical priest.

What was rejected has now been accepted without reproach or unworthiness. From Adokimos to Aamometos (with parentage, sons)

Jesus has become the way of escape! Now we are to work out our soul salvation in fear and trembling according to Philippians 2:13-15. Are you working out your soul salvation or busy trying to work out someone else's;by finding fault? You and I have no stones to throw at each other, because we are all equal in his sight (redeemed from the curse of the law of sin and death). So, you still think you're ready for the wedding. The greatest wedding you and I will ever attend and be the honorees at is the one to the Lamb our Bride Groom. Marry Him first, and the rest will follow!

We are to reflect on the inside "the blameless and harmless" nature of sons without rebuke. What was legally rejected and lost, physically, and divinely has been restored to its rightful position. This is why we are to be merciful towards each other, because we were once without mercy.

James 2:13, 'show mercy that there maybe mercy for you at the judgment. Not boasters of self, vain-glorious in II Peter 2:17, Jude 1:12 as fountains or clouds that promise water, but deceive those who rely on them.' Boastful deceivers and seducers is what we had to offer before the cross!

We are to stare Satan down, see Acts 27:15, as a ship (an eye) bearing up against the wind, staring the storm in the face. (Hebrews 4:15) Ready to reap the reward of the whirlwind.

Hebrews 12, 13 shows us Jesus taking us outside the temple walls and gates, as they did in the Old Testament with the Lamb that was to be offered on the Day of Atonement, and commanding us to die. While we are outside before we confess salvation, we cannot claim our inheritance. When we die daily, we receive more of the inheritance and some of the extra perks for just being willing and obedient. He said that not only will we withdraw our blessings from our inheritance, but also they would chase us down and overtake us as we go along our daily business. We must enter this realm of blessedness from the New

Covenant (the inside/hidden relationship with him). We have so many examples throughout the Bible of the lives that were unhidden (outside) and hidden (inside) Christ. Note the man at the Gate Beautiful, Abraham & Sarah, Hannah, Anna (Mary's' mother), Joseph, John the Baptist, Peter, Potiphar, Samuel and Jeconiah, Samson, Jezebel, Jonah, David, Miriam, Tobias and Tamar.

Those who were on the outside were headless (Ichabod) and subject to self with the penalty of death as its reward. All were used mightily of God when they made the decision to come inside and gain the position of headship. Let's look at what it is like to be without a head (Ichabod).

Ichabod

Ichabod was the son of Phinehas and grandson of Eli the High Priest. His father Phinehas contaminated the Temple of the Lord without constraint and was not corrected by the High Priest; which happened to be his Father. It was not the failings of a father that cost him the lives of his sons and ultimately his own, but the failings of the High Priest of Gods' House to judge in righteousness. God raised up the Prophet Samuel to bring warning before destruction "1 Samuel 3:11 And the LORD said to Samuel, Behold, I will do a thing in Israel, at which both the ears of every one that heareth it shall tingle. 12 In that day I will perform against Eli all things which I have spoken concerning his house: when I begin, I will also make an end. 13 For I have told him that I will judge his house for ever for the iniquity which he knoweth; because his sons made themselves vile, and he restrained them not. 14 And therefore I have sworn unto the house of Eli, that the iniquity of Eli's house shall not be purged with sacrifice nor offering for ever. "

When God has expectations for your life nothing short of its fulfillment is sufficient! We all operate in offices also known as elections and callings, and they are without repentance. You may delay responding to them but they are never simply null and void unless you play with God like Eli did! The results of Eli's disobedience to God in caring for the Temple without respect of persons cost him a lot!

I Samuel 4:19 And his daughter in law, Phinehas' wife, was with child, near to be delivered: and when she heard the tidings that the ark of God was taken, and that her father in law and her husband were dead, she bowed herself and travailed; for her pains came upon her. 20 And about the time of her death the women that stood by her said unto her, Fear not; for thou hast born a son. But she answered not, neither did she regard it. 21 And she named the child Ichabod, saying, The glory is departed from Israel: because the ark of God was taken, and because of her father in law and her husband. 22 And she said, The glory is departed from Israel: for the ark of God is taken.

Those who ignore the supreme authority of God even though they occupy an office are doing so without a covering. This stiff-necked rebelliousness walks in self-denial and self-justification of the sins that are before their very eyes! Thus the people they lead are often led astray and ultimately left without endued authority to lead spiritually in their homes or congregations! Ichabod became a byproduct word for one who is headless! Without a head there is no authority over the body!

He is either Lord of all or Lord of none according to David in Psalms 24:1-10 "1 The earth is the LORD'S, and the fulness thereof; the world, and they that dwell therein. 2 For he hath founded it upon the seas, and established it upon the floods. 3 Who shall ascend into the hill of the LORD? or who shall stand in his holy place? 4 He that hath clean hands, and a pure heart; who hath not lifted up his soul unto vanity, nor sworn deceitfully. 5 He shall receive the blessing from the LORD, and righteousness from the

God of his salvation. 6 This is the generation of them that seek him, that seek thy face, O Jacob. Selah.7 Lift up your heads, O ye gates; and be ye lift up, ye everlasting doors; and the King of glory shall come in. 8 Who is this King of glory? The LORD strong and mighty, the LORD mighty in battle. 9 Lift up your heads, O ye gates; even lift them up, ye everlasting doors; and the King of glory shall come in. 10 Who is this King of glory? The LORD of hosts, he is the King of glory. Selah."

Ascension Requires Submission

To enter into his gates with thanksgiving and into his courts with praise we must meet the prerequesites:
This question is asked in Who shall ascend into the hill of the LORD? or who shall stand in his holy place?

- clean hands
- pure heart
- not lifted up his soul unto vanity
- or sworn deceitfully

When they are met God says that he"…will receive the blessing from the LORD, and righteousness from the God of his salvation…this is the generation of them that seek him, that seek thy face, O Jacob. Selah." Access has now been granted!

Ephesians 2:14-18

For He Himself is our peace, who has made both one, and has broken down the middle wall of separation, having abolished in His flesh the enmity, that is, the law of commandments contained in ordinances, so as to create in Himself one new man from the two, thus making peace, and that he might reconcile them both to God in one body through the cross, thereby putting to death the enmity. And he came and preached peace to you who were afar off and to those who were near. For through Him we both have access by one Spirit to the Father. (NKJV)

John 1:1-4, 12-14

In the beginning was the Word, and the Word was with God, and the Word was God. He was in the beginning with God. All things were made through Him, and without Him nothing was made that was made. In Him was life, and the life was the light of men. And the light shines in the darkness, and the darkness did not comprehend it…

But as many as received Him, and the world did not know Him. He came to His own, and His own did not receive Him. But as many as received Him, to them He gave the right to become children of God, to those who believe in

His name: who were born, not of blood, nor of the will of the flesh, nor of the will of man, but of God. And the Word became flesh and dwelt among us, and we beheld His glory, the glory as of the only begotten of the Father, full of grace and truth.

Hebrews 12:5-29

And you have forgotten the exhortation which speaks to you as to sons: My son, do not despise the chastening of the Lord, Nor be discouraged when you are rebuked by Him; For whom the Lord loves He chastens, And scourges every son whom He receives. If you endure chastening, God deals with you as with sons, for what son is there whom a father does not chasten? But if you are without chastening, of which all have become partakers, then you are illegitimate and not sons. We have had human fathers who corrected us, and we paid them respect. Shall we not much more readily be in subjection to the Father of the spirits and live? For they indeed for a few days chastened us as seemed best to them, but he for our profit, that we may be partakers of His holiness. Now no chastening seems to be joyful for the present, but painful, nevertheless, afterward it yields the peaceable fruit of righteousness to those who have been trained by it.

Therefore strengthen the hands which hang down, and the feeble knees, and make straight paths for your feet, so that what is lame may not be dislocated, but rather be healed. Pursue peace with all people, and holiness, without which no one will see the Lord: looking carefully lest anyone fall short of the grace of God; lest any root of bitterness springing up cause trouble, and by this many become defiled; lest there be any fornicator or profane person like Esau, who for one morsel of food sold his birthright.

For you know that afterward, when we wanted to inherit the blessing, he was rejected, for he found no place for repentance, though he sought it diligently with tears. For you have not come to the mountain that may be touched and that burned with fire, and to blackness and darkness and tempest, and the sound of a trumpet and the voice of words, so that those who heard it begged that the word should not be spoken to them anymore. (For they could not endure what was commanded: And if so much as a beast touches the mountain, it shall be stoned or shot with an arrow." And so terrifying was the sight that Moses said, "I am exceedingly afraid and trembling.")

But you have come to Mount Zion and to the city of the living God, the heavenly Jerusalem, to an innumerable company of angels, to the general assembly and church of the firstborn who are registered in heaven, to God the Judge of all, to the spirits of just men made perfect, to Jesus the Mediator of the new covenant, and the blood of sprinkling speaks better things than that of Abel.

See that you do not refuse Him who speaks. For if they did not escape who refused Him who spoke on earth, much more shall we not escape if we turn away from Him who speaks from heaven, whose voice then shook the earth, but now He has promised, saying, "Yet once more I shake not only the earth, but also heaven." Now this, yet once more, "indicates the removal of those things that are being shaken, as of things that are made, that the things which cannot be shaken may remain. Therefore, since we are receiving a kingdom that cannot be shaken, let us have grace, by which we serve God acceptably with reverence and godly fear. For our God is a consuming fire.

Galatians 4:1-11

Now I say that the heir as long as he is a child, does not differ at all from a slave, though he is master of all, but his guardians and stewards until the time appointed by the father. Even so we, when we were children, were in bondage under the elements of the world.

When we were once in bondage under the elements of the world. But when the fullness of time had come, God sent forth His Son, born of a woman, born under the law, to redeem those who were under the law, that we might receive the adoption as sons. And because you are sons, God has sent forth the Spirit of His Son into your hearts, crying out, "Abba, Father!' Therefore you are no longer a slave but a son, and if a son, then an heir of God through Christ. But then, indeed, when you did not know God, you served those that by nature are not gods. But now after you have known God, or rather are known by God, how is it that you turn again to the weak and beggarly elements, to which you desire again to be in bondage? You observe days and months and seasons and years. I am afraid for you, lest I have labored for you in vain.

Romans 10:3

For they being ignorant of God's righteousness, and seeking to establish their own righteousness, has not submitted to the righteousness of God. Christ is the end of the law for righteousness to everyone who believes. For Moses wrote about the righteousness which is of the law, "The man who does those things shall live by them." But the righteousness of faith speaks in this way, "Do not say in your heart, "…who will ascend into heaven?" (That is, to bring Christ down from above) or, "who will descend into the abyss?" (That is, to bring Christ up from the dead). But what does it say? "The word is near you, in your mouth and in your heart" (that is, the word of faith which we preach): that if you confess with your mouth the Lord Jesus and believe in your heart that God raised Him from the dead, you will be saved.

For with the heart one believes, has relationship unto righteousness, and with the mouth confession is made unto salvation. For the Scripture says, "Whoever believes on Him will not be put to shame. For there is no distinction between the Jew and Greek, for the same Lord over all is rich to all who call upon Him. For "whoever calls on the name of the Lord shall be saved."

James 4:1-10

Where do wars and fights come from among you? Do they not come from your desires for pleasure that war in your members? You lust and do not have. You murder and covet and cannot obtain. You fight and war. Yet you do not have because you do not ask. You ask and do not receive, because you ask amiss, that you may spend it on pleasures. Adulterers and adulteresses! Do you not know that friendship with the world is enmity with God? Whoever therefore wants to be a friend of the world makes himself an enemy of God. Or do you think that the Scripture says in vain, "The Spirit who dwells in us yearns jealously"? But He gives more grace, Therefore He says: "God resist the proud, But gives grace to the humble." Therefore submit to God. Resist the devil and he will flee from you.

Draw near to God and He will draw near to you. Cleanse your hands, you sinners; and purify your hearts, you double-minded. Lament and mourn and weep! Let your laughter be turned to mourning and your joy to gloom. Humble yourselves in the sight of the Lord, and He will lift you up.

Satan's anointing rode us like a wet blanket before salvation. As an anointed cherub in heaven, he had God's holy anointing. His anointing has been perverted, polluted and empowered by the works of the flesh. This is why Satan accuses us with our past, because it is his past that keeps him locked into the position of defeat by God. Our defeat fuels his passion and power!

God commands us to forget those things which are behind so that his anointing keeps us victorious and in relationship.

My Father and I are one! It is the self-same anointing in us that quickened Christ from the dead! I recall one year a portion of a radio broadcast quoting an interview given to a world wide news media on a celebrity. In the article this celebrity spoke of how they hated themselves. I was dressing for work, and God began to reveal to me why Satan has a grip on suicide as a tool to destroy lives. He has perverted the truth. If any man would follow me, let him deny himself. To die is gain…I die daily…It is no longer I that lives but, Christ that lives in me…I in him, I move, live and have my being…all things exist in him and through him.

When an individual is despairing of himself, he feels the only answer is to be free of him self. So to do this he must kill his body and cease to be an issue or source of pain to himself or others. This is a signal that there is a need for freedom, but the answer eludes the natural mind. How?

Satan uses his tools of perversion to cloud the mind. But the answer that disperses the cloud of confusion is a true and personal relationship with Jesus Christ.

All of the other volumes of the books of the Bible have been to bring you to this point and that you have seen the diasporas of life through the word of God. We are now into maintaining your freedom. To do this requires a relationship with one who is able to relate to us as we are, right where we are, right when we need him. All we have to do is reach out to Him with these words "Come into my heart any make me over in your image."

A new life and identity just like Gideon.' His name meant to be "cut down." A surrendering of the heart is what is done in the hidden part. To rend the garment and not the heart is a form of pride and an outward show of self. God requires us to make a private place for him, so that he can demonstrate as he chooses, when he chooses. This is liberty that moves in God as we are drawn into his presence. Drawing nigh to God will bring us into Jubilee. Released from the debts of the past years the fulfillment of the covenant (manifesting) the evidence of life whose debts have been cancelled.

We proclaim (prophesy) it and He "God" will establish it. God said that he hastens to perform his word. Through that performance a supernatural unity is created and the favor of the Lord enshrouds us. Surrounds as the mountains surround Jerusalem, so the Lord surrounds his people with the kind of favor that releases us from prison. Pushes us back into the posture of what God originally designed or us before Adam's fall. All or our senses become new: ears, eyes and vocals – to hear, see and speak as he directs. Senses that alert to and recognize the voice of the good shepherd. Running to be in his presence, and stand strong in the anointing. Strong in the Hebrew is Astam; meaning in body in Psalms 139:14 –

Al Novak, states in Hebrew Honey, "That is, the human body which is wonderfully made and is composed of a million projects bound together." As we abide in the presence of the Holy of Holies we are sustained, established, planted and firm in our places. The more we worship the Holy One, the more we become God conscious instead of sin conscious. This revelation produces Jubilee. With our senses heightened to be on cue to hearken (hear and obey) our supernatural strength allows us to know things before they happen. Even too while they are happening.

There is a pattern to be taken notice of here – As our sin debts have been supernaturally cancelled, we too must supernaturally cancel the sin debts that others owe us. Injuries to our emotional, physical, and financial health. Understand I am speaking of forgiveness. Many will never be able to pay you back for emotional, and physical pain. Once you have been injured a scar occurs in its place. It requires the salve of forgiveness to penetrate beneath the scabs and bruises to bring true healing. Even financially, you may sue or get repaid, but the strain of the loss is felt long after.

God has painted us with the anointed fragrance of the undefiled blood of his son in Luke 4, and God is attracted to the sweet smell of sacrifice. He in turn is compelled to pour out his free favor on us. This blood is whole; it does not carry the illnesses of the curse. Therefore, there is no stench. Unlike the blood of animals and man, that carries the stench of active curses. That blood carries an obtrusive odor. The components are entangled with the components of death; sickness and disease.

Jesus has shown himself strong on our behalf, bringing us out of the stench of death and obscurity. It is like 'Honey in the Rock" – the revelation knowledge revealed through

Jesus, His Blood, His Anointing and His Word.

Jesus has become our way of escape, our door out of the land of Egypt, and our compass through the wilderness, and our securer of the promises in the Promise Land. In I Corinthians 10:11-13, it is stated "Now all these things happened unto them for ensamples: and they are written for our admonition, upon whom the ends of the world are come. Wherefore let him that thinketh that he standeth take heed lest he fall. There hath no temptation taken you but such as is common to man: but God is faithful, who will not suffer you to be tempted above that ye are able, but will with the temptation also make a way to escape, that ye may be able to bear it."

All of our problems must be faced with the knowledge that where the Son is there is Liberty through his anointing. No matter what we face, God through his Son Jesus has been broken the authority of it for us. We simply have to receive and work the authority that has been given us over death, hell and the grave through intimate love with the triune personhood of God.

Beth Moore, in "Things Pondered" expounds on I Corinthians 13:8. "Love never fails"…"Does it never fail the giver or the receiver?" It fails neither. For the receiver they will never have been loved for nothing. God is very practical. If he has called upon you to be His vessel of love toward someone else it is because He has a plan ... Love never fails the Giver ... He never "fails" to make the unlovely lovely to you ... There will be times that it will break our hearts to be vessels of God's love toward another, but its ultimate end is meant for salvation. The salvation of someone's soul, health, reputation, marriage, honor, sanity. Through love He saves spirit, soul, mind and body"

We must first present our bodies as a living sacrifice, no longer a need to die the death of the cross for our sins. He has taken our place, but not removed the responsibility of offering ourselves as offerings in the use of kingdom business. We are to be with clean hands and a pure heart, have your hands shed innocent blood or served with ulterior motives? Clean your hands through the washing of the water of the word; apply the word of God to the sins committed by the hands. Purify your heart with the fire of the word through the refiners fire and the habitation of the Holy Spirit pressing out the old man and writing the heart of God into your heart! Repent of seeking the hand of God above the face of God and of any means by which you have decieved yourself or others.

CHAPTER 2

The War of the Cross!

"Satan has nothing in us, except the things we have not repented of and surrendered! These dark things he can work on us with! Because Satan found no shadow or turning in Jesus, he had nothing on Him to defeat Him! God's law is sure and perfect converting the heart! He does not have to do anything else, because it has already been done. Our role is to apply what has been done! Everything is set. Jesus was driven into the wilderness and came out with victory established for us! The Old Testament Saints could not walk in victory because of what Satan had in them. We are New Testament Saints and we are heirs to the victory Jesus established!

Reference: I Corinthians 2:2 & I Peter 2:21-25

The War of The Cross

2- Our Lives before the Cross

Destined for death, hell and the grave! But God! Extricated us from the clutches of death, hell and the grave. Meaning we were unraveled -- distinguished from a related thing; freed or removed from entanglement or difficulty.

Similar meanings for extricate are disentangle, untangle, disencumber, disembarrass – to free from what binds or holds back. We were spiritually and physically bound hand, foot, mouth, ears, arms and mentally by the law of sin and death. How can a house be taken over unless the strong comes in and binds up the owner? Satan came in and bound us spiritually so he could control us physically.

All dressed up in grave clothes like Lazarus, and confined to a place full of the living stinking dead.

The source of your spirit will either build you up or tear you down. Eugene Peterson's Message Translation of James 5:1-6, reads as follows: "…and a final word to you arrogant rich. Take some lessons in lament. You'll need buckets for the tears when the crash comes upon you. Your money is corrupt and your fine clothes stink. Your greedy luxuries are a cancer in your gut, destroying your life from within. You thought you were piling up wealth what you've piled up is judgment. All the workers you've exploited and cheated cry out for judgment. The groans of the workers you used and abused are a roar in the ears of the Master Avenger. You've looted the earth and lived it up.

But all you'll have to show for it is a fatter than usual corpse. In fact, what you've done is condemn and murder perfectly good persons, who stand there and take it."

This is proof that the life you live if it is not consecrated to God is of nothing and is vanity.

Romans 3:3-4 says, "For what if some did not believe? Shall their unbelief make the faith of God without effect? God forbid: yea, let God be true, but every man a liar; as it is written, That thou mightest be justified in thy sayings, and mightest overcome when thou art judged."

As unbelievers we were confined to a place of bondage known as death, hell and the grave!

We were under the curse of the Law, it was weighing heavily on top of us, and we were constantly falling. Failing to finish the course before us caught up in the world and its devices. It would require a war being fought and won by one who is incapable of being defeated to gain and secure our liberty forever. That is why the battle is not ours but the Lords. People war against each other, because they can defeat one another. But when God enters a battle there can be only one victor -- because he has all power. Not requiring the assistance of temporal weapons, there is of no record a battle lost when God was in it.

War in the Greek is polemeo - to war, make war, fight, followed by kata against, to contend, quarrel. Our bodies and its' members warred against itself and we were in need of perfected peace! Have you noticed how some families hurt each other more than anyone on the outside could or would ever think to do? Medical history records exactly 39 main diseases of which other diseases have their root in. How many stripes did Jesus receive -- forty save one; equals 39. For every stripe on his back the victory was won over those roots. Satan had nothing in him or on him. That is why there was no contest or discussion when Jesus entered into hell. Satan smelled defeat even before Jesus went into the pit. The moment Jesus entered the pit -- Satan did not resist -- he surrendered and ran. How do I know that? The Bible says resist the Devil and he will flee! Jesus resisted, and guess who had to flee! We needed peace and Jesus gave it!

The Greek words for peace from war meant to have peace within, to live peaceably, to make peace, to be in accord, agree to reconcile. The Hebrew word is Shalam, meaning to be whole, sound, safe, completed, finished, ended to repay, to impart prosperity.

The war had been raging since Genesis 3, when God pronounced that there would be hostility between the seed of the woman (Adam) and the seed of the serpent (Satan). A great drama was consummated by the seed of the woman (Jesus) that climaxed in the seed of the serpent (Satan) being conquered. We have been given the victory and the power to sustain our victory. Before Jesus could not abide in us, and neither could we defeat Satan with the temporal sacrifice of the blood of bullocks and goats. We needed a High Priest who did not need to be replaced because of his own sins, but one who could administer the plan of God continually. One who shall never be replaced, he was and is without sin!

The prophecy of this wars beginning and ending was prophesied by God in Genesis 3:15, and Revelation 6:19 respectively.

The judgment God pronounced on Satan was that he would eat the dust.

Then God reminded Adam and Eve that they were that dust! So Satan feasts on mankind as long as mans' nature is dusty -- carnal. Whatever is that dust? What we choose to hold onto and not surrender to God. The carnal areas of our lives provide a 24-7 feasting and resting-place for Satan. Now Jesus has placed all things under his feet, and even the very clouds are the dusts of Jesus' feet.

So why do we often blame God and Satan for the things that are wrong in our lives? Remember we were shapen and born in iniquity and dressed in dust suits. So, until we accept the water of the word we remain dust. We, become the original red clay of Eden (Paradise) when we accept the water of the word into our dusty souls. We are returned to our original state of authority. Adam's name meant red earth, having will that was pliable. As clay is responsive in the hands of the potter so are our souls when we return to that original state of existing totally dependent on God.

We must realize that instead of blaming God or Satan we need to look at our own reflection in the mirror. Francis Frangipane writes about tells a cardinal he observed one day. Francis noticed how the cardinal was very territorial, and would fight off other cardinals. The cardinal began to attack another cardinal, so he thought; but the cardinal was attacking his reflection in the chrome bumper of Francis's car. God revealed to Francis that this is how we are our own enemy.

Dust we are and dust we shall return one day. We must dust off our souls and place them under the water of the word. When must look at ourselves and see the real us. A portrait painted with a brush dipped in the color of our life of sin that has made us what we are. The brokeness of that life has darkened the recesses of our soul. It is this sin nature within us that drives us into the arms of temporary comfort; that adulterous affair, that fornicating moment, that bottle of booze, pills or needles of damnation. Maybe you never did any of theses things, but you did other things. Maybe you consider yourself a good person. I want you to know that there are a lot of good people in hell, and on their way to hell. Good is not good enough. You are in need of a saviour! I pray you know Jesus Christ in the pardon of your sins.

No matter what the sin, we were all the children of Satan at one time or another. We were constantly disobedient and under his control. Our old nature worked hard at keeping us in the will of Satan. He kept a firm grasp on our every move. If our flesh thought a thing, he made sure we had access to it. But now Jesus, is our power supply of Salvation. He is the Dustbuster of our dusty souls. The Blood, the Word, and the Holy Spirit are our other cleaning tools that get into those hard to reach crevices and corners.

It is those areas of the soul that cause us to be hard-hearted. Refusing to admit how vulnerable we are -- like free-range chicken -- game for the attacks of Satan. Our self-righteous behavior flaunts itself in the spirit of one-upsmanship. We tell ourselves we are not like so and so, and we are alright. To paraphrase Francis Frangipane, who said we must know what is in us, and who is in us if we are to be successful in our war against the devil? To war effectively we must separate what is of the flesh from what is of the devil. We must ask ourselves, are the things oppressing us today the harvest of what we planted yesterday?"

The Bible tells us to agree quickly with thine adversary lest at any time the adversary deliver us to the judge and we be cast into prison. The adversary occupies the dust of our soul. Jesus is telling us that since Satan tells part of the truth, acknowledge the truth he speaks and denounce the lies.

Remind him that because of who Jesus is our righteousness and he died for our imperfect flesh, and through his blood we are forgiven and cleansed. Remind Satan, that you stand before the throne of Grace. Submitted to God and you are being perfected into the image of God.

What you just did was use a couple of the vital keys to overcoming Satan. One key is called the Key of Humility. Another the Key of Virtue -- being pleasing to God. Repenting of our sins instead of hiring ourselves out as our defense attorney. Confront Satan with the power of salvation. Jesus has defended us and of not guilty has been rendered and the case is closed.

Humility (Kana in Hebrew) means to bend the knee, fold together packages, bundles, and wares. A man, who submits himself to the Lord, bends his knee, folds together the packages of his weaknesses and wares and presents them at the feet of Jesus. So that he may become a package pleasing to the Lord. Willing to be sent and open by those whom God sends us to as gifts wherever the Lord wills (excerpt from Hebrew Honey, page 135, Al Novak).

Remember how Satan fears virtue, and he is terrified of humility. He hates it because these two areas are what Jesus used to defeat him in hell. Jesus humbled himself, and became obedient even unto death and showed forth the virtue of the one who had sent him. To be like Jesus means we must travel this same path to victory. To be in relationship with someone means you agree with him or her. How? By walking in the same mind as them. Enoch walked with God and he was no more. Enoch was no more. He no longer existed outside of God, but in God -- therefore they became inseparable. Selah (Pause and think about it)

'How can two walk together except they be agreed.' Satan hates virtue and humility, because it is the surrender of your dusty soul to Jesus to be Lord and Saviour over. It is the stronghold of the Godly -- the consistently righteous run into him and are safe!

Through the sins of our own souls reflection we see the good and the evil if we are true to ourselves. The light and the dark are clearly defined. The question before us is can a Christian be assailed and tormented by Satan? The answer is yes. Can a Christian be demon possessed? I use to believe this was an emphatic no. But, now I do believe that part of their soul can be controlled. Not possessed, because we are the possessions of God. But he can still reside as a trespasser if we have not evicted him, and if we tend to toy with the dark. Whatever the measure of darkness exist in our life so the measure of Satan's access is in us. Remember he was given legal access to dwell in the outer recesses of darkness. Likewise to the measure of light in your life so is the measure of God's access through Jesus.

The Bible says light and darkness have no fellowship with the other. Accordingly the things and people that surround a person and those they fellowship with can determine the nature of a person. Key scripture -- remember the light shone in the darkness and it comprehended it not. But still the light of the world has overcome darkness. The position of being over is not under. Light is over, and dark is under. God is over all. And Satan is where under his feet. He made us against our sin nature to be the head and not the tail, above only and not beneath.

We are going to follow this principle out line upon line, and precept upon precept. Are you Ready, let's go!

Peter's denial of Jesus came as a result of his tolerance of darkness in his life. And because the darkness was present Satan made a demand to have permission to sift him like wheat.

Luke 22:31-32, says "Simon, Simon, behold, Satan has demanded permission to sift you like wheat..."Satan gained permission because there was something of Satan inside of

Peter. Let's look at the point of entry. Satan can't come in unless we extend the invitation. The invitation is darkness and pride. When we yield to the dark the door opens, and he steps in. The door was competition. We find them both 8 verses prior to verse 24, "And they began to question among themselves, which of them should be considered the greatest. Of course Peter deemed himself the greatest, because he was the water-walking disciple! He just knew he was the greatest! Then 30 verses later Peter is sifted by Satan.

Luke 11:35, Jesus says "Take heed, that the light which is in you be not in, darkness." Warning comes before destruction! This was almost 10 chapters earlier.

So, first the warning from the Holy Spirit comes that there is darkness in our hearts. The Holy Spirit comes from God through Jesus, and it is of that undefiled spirit that Jesus pours out himself upon all flesh. Then the thief took notice and desired to come in. Then the door of Peter's heart opened because of his fellowship with the darkness of pride and competition. The gate of his soul was left unguarded. The thief knew that there was more darkness in Peter than light at the moment of temptation. Why was that? Wasn't Peter born again? Yes, but not yet empowered. If you have been wrestling with the idea of why you need to be filled with the Holy Spirit -- then this ought to resolve the issue. Just stop and ask Jesus to fill you with the Holy Spirit right now! I believe that you are receiving it right now! That the manifestation of the presence will flow freely from the depths of your belly, in Jesus Name, Amen! Faith cometh by hearing and hearing by the word of God! May you forever be changed into the brightness of his express image. Just open your mouth and begin to exercise your new language -- don't think about what to say just allow the pressure cap to break and speak!

Peter was lacking in courage at the time of his temptation, because darkness weakened him. Now wasn't this the same Peter who had cut off the guards' ear earlier in the garden! You see darkness weakens even the strongest among us. Peter later humbled himself and repented of having had this darkness in himself.

If we allow darkness to remain we allow ourselves to be used like a mense cloth. Satan has legal access to the dark. Pride was the area of darkness in Peter's heart that opened the door. Proverbs 16:18, says "Pride goeth before destruction, and an haughty spirit before a fall.

So it wasn't all Satan's fault, he is a true opportunist -- he capitalized on the moment at hand -- which is his nature.

Proverbs 15:29 says, "The Lord is for the wicked; (those that practice and plan to do evil) but he heareth the prayer of the righteous (those that practice and plan to do right).

Our strength is found in submission. James 5:7-8 says "Submit yourselves therefore to God. Resist the devil, and he will flee from you." Draw nigh to God, and he will draw nigh to you. Cleanse your hands, ye sinners; and purify your hearts, ye double-minded." A sinner is someone who practices and plans to do evil, but a righteous person practices and plans to do right.

In case we are not clear on what is wickedness; let's observe a wicked person in scripture. "James 4:1-5, Where do wars and fights come from among you? Do they not come from your desires for pleasure that war in your members? You lust and do not have. You murder and covet and cannot obtain. You fight and war. Yet you do not have because you do not ask. You ask and you do not receive, because you ask amiss, that you may spend it on your pleasures. Adulterers and adulteresses! Do you not know that friendship with the world is enmity (war, italics mine) with God? Whoever therefore wants to be a friend of the world makes himself an enemy of God. Or do you think that the scripture says in vain, "The spirit who dwells in us yearns jealously?" But he gives more grace. Therefore, He says "God resists the proud, But gives grace to the humble."

The Prince of Darkness made sure we lived a life devoted to being led by our own passions and different lusting. In other words our occupation was that of a sinner. Some of us were Specialist in the field(s) of lust, witchcraft and false worship, anger and gluttony.

Some of the occupations had sub-job headings, and I have outlined the fields of specialty and their job headings.

These areas of strongholds are habits of sin in a person's life. The sin habit is a dwelling place that will rob you of your power and your joy.

Sins of the Eye

- Adultery, unlawful sex between married persons other than their mates, and with unmarried persons.
- Fornication, sex between unmarried persons.
- Uncleanness, homosexuality, pornography, masturbation, erotic fantasies, bestiality, rape, incest, and exploitation and raping of children.
- Lasciviousness, out of control desires and lewd behavior, acting out lewd fantasies.

Sins of Divination and False Worship

- Idolatry, worship of statues, pictures and images.
- Witchcraft, conjuring up evil spirits to communicate with and through, spells, charms, amulets worn on the body or clothing to ward off or welcome the presence of evil spirits. Inflicting evil upon others through enchantments, or to control ones behavior for or against persons.

Sins of Anger

- Hatred, bitter dislike, abhorrence, ill thoughts and hopes on others. Holding grudges.
- Variances, dissension, discord, quarreling, debating and dispute.
- Emulation's, jealousies, competition.
- Wrath, rage and anger that lingers. Turmoil and vengeance that is sought.
- Strife, words, and the intent to pay back in kind the wrong done to them.
- Sedition's, cliques, stirring up junk and mess everywhere they go.
- Heresies, will not accept the Truth, but has own

private interpretation. Divisive and group forming to pull away from true believers in Christ Jesus.

- Envying, jealousy and ill will at the good fortune of others.
- Murders', destroying the happiness of others with lies, and gossip. Actual taking of a life of another human being.

Sins of Gluttony

- Drunkenness always in excess and bondage to sex, alcohol and/or drugs.
- Reveling, riots, obscenities and uninhibited feasting and partying.
- The components of sin are rooted in the authority of division.

Components of Sin

| Power of Sin | By the blood |
| Guilt of Sin | Through the blood |

Now in James 4:7-12 let's observe the righteous. Lament and mourn and weep. Let your laughter be turned into mourning and your joy to gloom. Humble yourselves in the sight of the Lord, and He will lift you up. Do not speak evil of one another, brethren. He who speaks evil of a brother and judges his brother, speaks evil of the law and judges the law. But if you judge the law, and are not a doer of the law but a judge. There is one Lawgiver, who is able to save and to destroy. Who are you to judge another."(NKJV)

It is whom you walk with and where you walk with them that determines who and what you agree with. You are known by the company you keep.

Now that we are clear, and the line of distinction has been drawn between dark and light. Who's on the Lord's side! How do we maintain the territory gained for us by the Captain of the Host -- Jehovah Tseboath?

By bringing every thought captive and walking (living) in Christian virtue.

These virtues are found in Philippians 4:8-9 "Finally brethren whatsoever things are true...honest...just...pure...lovely...of good report; if there be any virtue, and if there be any praise, think on these things." Those things, which ye have both learned ...received ...heard...seen in me do: and the God of peace shall be with you."

Colossians 2:6,7,9 says, "As ye have therefore received Christ Jesus the Lord so walk ye in him. Rooted and built up in him and stablished in the faith, as ye have been taught, abounding therein with thanksgiving...For in him dwelleth all the fulness of the Godhead bodily. And ye are complete in him, which is the head of all principality and power...in putting off the body of the sins of the flesh by the circumcision of Christ: Buried with him in baptism wherein also ye are risen with him through the faith of the operation of God, who hath raised him from the dead. And you being dead in your sins and the uncircumcision of your flesh, hath he quickened together with him, having forgiven you all trespasses. Blotting out the handwriting of ordinances that was against us, and took it out of the way, nailing it to the cross; and having spoiled principalities and powers, he made a shew of them openly, triumphing over them in it."

In Colossians 2:1-16 "If ye then be risen with Christ, seek those things which are above, where Christ sitteth on the right hand of God. Set your affection on those things above, not on things on the earth. For ye are dead, and your life is hid with Christ in God. When Christ, who is our life, shall appear, then shall ye also appear with him in glory. Mortify therefore your members, which are upon the earth; fornication, uncleanness, inordinate affection, and concupiscence (lust of the eyes, deceitful, youthful lust of sensual objects, pleasures, profits and honors) and covetousness, which is idolatry. For which things...the wrath of God cometh on the children of disobedience; … which ye walked some time, when ye lived in them. But now…put off all these; anger, wrath, malice, blasphemy, filthy communication out of your mouth…seeing that ye have put off the old man…and have put on the new man…Put on therefore, is the elect of God, holy and beloved, bowels of mercies; kindness, humbleness of mind, meekness, longsuffering, forbearing one another and forgiving one another, if any man have a quarrel against any; even as Christ forgave you, so also do ye. And above all these things put on charity (love), which is the bond of perfectness. And let the peace of God rule in your hearts, to the which also ye are called in one body…Let the word of Christ dwell in you…"

John W. Ritenbaugh says the following of God's desires toward Israel as his chosen people, "The Sovereignty of God (Part 1)Now this word "to know"--yada in Hebrew, ginöskö in Greek--indicates a combination of close, warm, and even passionate intimacy, combined with head knowledge that produces an edge in a person's life that enables him to trust God and at the same time perceive what He is doing. It is this factor that makes God's Word have authority with us. We know Him. It is not just a casual acquaintance, and it forms the very foundation of a true working relationship. We need to ask ourselves: Do we really believe that God is holy, and because of that, His anger burns against sin; that because He is righteous, His judgments fall on those who rebel; that because He is faithful, His promises of either blessings or curses are absolute; that because He is omnipotent, nobody can resist Him; and because He is omniscient, there is no problem of which He is unaware or cannot master? Because God is what He is, we are seeing the prophecies He inspired regarding the end of the age being fulfilled in the world and in the church, and that translates into tumultuous, difficult, and sometimes scary and even confusing times for us." Amos 3:3 says "Can two walk together, except they be agreed?" John W. Ritenbaugh further states, "Can two exist in a marriage relationship where one is constantly unfaithfully acting as a harlot? Yet, of all the nations that have existed on the earth, the only one that God made a covenant with did this to Him. God entered into no other relationship with any other nation in all of the history of mankind. A person may have many friends, many family members, many business friends, fraternal friends, professional relationships, but by biblical standards for marriage, it is one spouse until death.

Intimacy with God and Israel's relationship involved an intimacy normally associated only within marriage. Yes, God had relationships with other nations, but none even close to what He had with Israel. It was favored with gifts greater than any nation because of that intimacy, but perhaps the greatest gift of all was the revelation of God Himself, the knowledge of His purpose, and how to live life at its fullest. But because of these gifts, Israel's responsibility and deviancy was also the greatest on earth: great Jerusalem, great deviancy. The gift had never been given to any other people on earth...

...Matthew 7:21-23, These verses again show a vital key to understanding our relationship with Him: Our love for Him is merely a response to His initiative. By way of contrast, compare these to what Jesus says to those who are not called as their disobedience shows, but who masquerade as disciples, even as ministers, as if they really knew the Father and Son: Not everyone who says to Me, "Lord, Lord," shall enter the kingdom of heaven. Many will say to Me in that day, "Lord, Lord, have we not prophesied in Your name, cast out demons in Your name, and done many wonders in Your name?" And then I will declare to them, "I never knew you; depart from Me, you who practice lawlessness!"

Since He never knew them, is this not just another way of saying, "I never loved you"?"

Lest Ye Be Like the Fig Tree

Jesus journeyed into Bethany, whose name means the "House of Depression or Misery" prior to his visit to the fig tree. Jesus went to the fig tree from the city of depression and misery to get some of is healing fruit. The fig tree is known throughout history to have medicinal properties. The trees failure to bear fruit is seen as a great calamity as referenced in the Song of Songs 2:13 and Matthew 24:32.

Stages of the Fig Trees Life

Some of the fig trees symbolism that I would like to note are that the early or green fig symbolizes ripeness and are gathered in the month of June according to Isaiah 28:4. Most of them drop off the tree before they are perfected according to Revelation 6:13. The winter or unripe fig grows under the leaves and does not ripen at the normal season but hang upon the trees during winter. They can be found growing wild, and have been cultivated in Palestine since ancient times. The fig appears before the leaves. When the leaves appear and there is no fruit on the tree, it means it will be barren for that season according to Matthew 21:19 and

Song of Solomon 2:13. About the beginning of April the figs have had ample time to ripen.

When the Fruit forms after winter the leaves put forth as a sign of summer approaching. It was reasonable for Jesus to expect to eat fresh figs from the tree or at least be able to partake of the medicinal sap of the bark.

The ripe figs are gathered and kept in baskets. In the case of Hezekiah they are mentioned as key in his miraculous healing. So, why did Jesus curse the fig tree?

Because it stood in the presence, the very face of God denying the power of God locked within it to produce the required fruit at the required season. Like believers today who say what's my motivation, mediocre, doing just enough to get by, lukewarm and not seeking to fulfill the call of God. It requires a relationship to see the manifestation of your fruit. The face metaphorically means to be in the sight or in the mind and will, purpose of someone. See Luke 1:6,15,75; Luke 15:18,21, Acts 8:21, Romans 12:17, Psalms 5:9, and Psalms 19:15.

John W. Ritenbaugh says, "Eternal life is more than just endless life. The biblical eternal life includes power to produce quality living superabundantly far beyond merely existing forever. We should touch briefly on its sexual aspect. Genesis 4:1, 17, 25 each contain the Hebrew word yada'. It has a wide variety of possible applications, one of which is "to lie by man." In each case in Genesis 4, it is translated as "knew," since that is its basic meaning. The Hebrews used it to describe the sexual part of the relationship between husband and wife; thus, it suggests intimacy. When applied to God, it highlights not merely being acquainted with Him but, as we would say today, being "inside His head." The corresponding Greek word, ginosko, translated "know" in John 17:3, can be and is used in the same way as yada' in Hebrew (see Luke 1:34). To know God thus includes a wide range of mental, emotional, and experiential knowledge. The fruit of this intimacy includes love, reverence, obedience, honor, gratitude, and deep affection. We come to know Him as sovereign Ruler, Master, parent, brother, friend, Savior, and Lawgiver. We would never know this mixture of admirable qualities and authority without getting close to Him. They compel us to yield to Him with all of our heart while we strive to obey and glorify Him…this points to Jesus indicating that eternal life is not merely endless,…but that those who have it live intimately with God and conduct their lives as God does—otherwise, there would be no close intimacy with Him."

Barren Fig Tree and the Believer

It looks, feels and smells like a tree planted for the purpose of bearing fruit, a specific kind of fruit. What is your specialty/purpose in the kingdom?

The tree fit in with the landscape and times of the land. Like many believers in a church service. The tree was doing a good job of passing itself off as productive, until the one who knew all came along and examined it up close and in person. Are you trying to pass? But the smell of the tree gave it away. I have read that the fig tree is fragrant. The passerby's could see it was a fig tree and smell that it was a fig tree, but they had not stopped to see if it was productive beneath the covering of leaves. All dressed up and no substance. What can others see in you, if they got up close to you would they see that you were one of those what you see is what you get folk or are you just a fakin' passing the time away.

But more than anything else, that added injury to insult was that if it was not producing it had to not believe in itself as a fig tree. Many believers are like this having a form of godliness but denying the power thereof.

We are not to be of those who draw back, but like those who believed before us.

The issue of barrenness is confronted. If you have never read the story of Hannah -- look it up. God had shut up Hannah's womb, but he had not shut up the fig trees. There is mercy when God did it, but when we do it oops! Barrenness is what denial and doubt will produce. This tree was alongside the road, and the custom was to let the strangers that passed by eat and be refreshed from the fruit. This tree required cultivation. Someone was investing time in it. Just like the preacher or that loved one has invested time in you, and what do you have to show for it. The fig tree could not blame its' barrenness on the location, because God did not place it in the wilderness (desert) but in a lush green pasture. The tree couldn't blame it on the timing, because it was the right time, and place. No excuse. Maybe you have been in the wrong place, and in the wrong time because you have failed to be or remain where God wanted you to be. Even if you are in a church is it the church God has ordained for you to be a part of at this time. Remember there is a time and a season for all things. God will provide the direction, but we have to follow the leading.

An Illustration of the barren fig tree is likening to the mere professors of religion that debate and discuss the authenticity of the word. Sitting under one's own prosperity and peace as recorded in Matthew 21:19, Luke 13:6-7, I King 4:25, Micah 4:4, and Matthew 7:16

A Spiritual Application of the fig tree is likening to the Amorites; whose fruit was above and roots below ground. The roots were symbolic of the parents and the fruit are the children (Amos 2:9-15).

A revelation of the barren fig tree is found in it having the audacity to stand in the presence of Jesus and not have the sign expected in the season to be expected. It is a testimony against the believers of today who stand in the presence of God without any evidence in their lives, not how many people you have brought to church. But it is about yourself and your own house? The Bible says in Proverbs that a curse undeserved will not produce. So the fig tree was deserving of the curse.

We as believers come together and say we are standing on Holy Ground, but don't have the sign, expected in the time. We stand and look and smell like saints. But if we do not believe that Christ has risen from the dead. Then we are none of his. And if we do not believe that Christ can raise the dead today we are none of his. When we became Christians we passed from death into life by receiving his life in us. If we are afraid of seeing the dead risen, then we are none of his, nor should we confess salvation. Because salvation is redemption from death, hell and the grave. The first begotten of the dead stood at the mouth of a borrowed tomb and death got back and the dead in Christ were risen. Those dead in Christ were imputed as righteous, and when He got everybody that was righteous got up! The grave had no legal right to hold them and the saints of old had been waiting for an opportunity to get up. They were all seen walking through the city. Because the message in his mouth was "o death where is your sting, and o grave where is your victory."

If we have the audacity to deny the power of the resurrection then we are dead in our trespasses. And we still owe the death tax -- which is death. We have to believe that we have the power to raise the dead, in order to speak to the dead issues in our lives, and prophecy like Ezekiel to the dry bones and command them to live. We are none of his, we are anathema, against him. He gave us life from the grave so that we could walk in the power of the resurrection (His spirit being poured out upon all dead and stinking flesh)

The water of the word resurrects the dead. This chorus of a song that I heard Vicki Yohe sing is ringing out in my spirit "I am running, I am running, I am running to the mercy seat. Where Jesus is calling. He said his grace would cover me. His blood will flow freely it will provide the healing. I m running to the mercy seat."

This song echoes out the components of salvation that are rooted in the authority of unity (oneness).

Components of Salvation One(ness)

Redemption	Deliverance from the power and full acquittal of the guilt
Blessings	Instead of the curse of the Law of Sin which was death

The parable of the grain of wheat is a symbolism of division and unity. Unless the seed falls into the ground and dies it remains alone. A grain of wheat's husk represents the outward life, the wrapping of the flesh) and the seed inside of the grain represents the life of the seed. Until it is planted it remains alone, but once it falls into the soil and becomes one with the earth around it, and totally dependent on the nutrients of the soil to propel it to its purpose in life it is divided -- separated from its' purpose.

John 12:24 "Verily, verily, I say unto you, Except a corn of wheat fall into the ground and die, it abideth alone; but if it die, it bringeth forth much fruit."

The life of the spirit of Christ Jesus is the seed that is planted into the soil of our hearts. Unless that seed is allowed to die in us and go through the transformation of the crucifying of the flesh, the life of that seed will not be realized in the power of the resurrection will bring forth much fruit.

Our hearts are wholly dark without salvation. Before the seed of salvation was planted, we worked the works of the flesh and the one whose seed we carried -- Satan. Now that we are out of the dark and carrying the seed of the one whom chose us, and has sent us -- Jesus we work out our soul salvation with fear and trembling.

As we water the seed of Jesus Christ (the Word), and edify (prophesy) to his spirit within us through our prayer language our fruit is revealed bountifully. Scripture says that out of our bellies shall flow rivers of living water. And faith cometh by hearing and hearing by the word of the Lord. We must read the word and prophesy the word over our unsurrendered soulish life so that we can reach our full measure of faith that is hidden in Christ Jesus.

Francis Frangipane in the "The Three Battlegrounds," writes "If you will truly walk with Jesus, many areas of your thinking process will be exposed...You will see strongholds fall and victory come. But I must warn you, there will be pressure from your flesh, as well as from the demonic world itself, to minimize or ignore what God is requiring of you.

You may be tempted to surrender just a token sin or some minor fault, while allowing you main problems to remain entrenched and well hidden. Let us realize the energies we expend in keeping our sins secret are the actual "materials" of which a stronghold is made. The demon you are fighting is using your thoughts to protect his access to your life."

Think about the areas of your life that God revealed any of the above, and write down the sins that you continue to commit, since you have been saved. Then pray this prayer adapted from Francis Frangipane, calling those sins audibly when you reach them...

"Heavenly Father, there are areas in my life (audibly name the habitual sins) that I have not fully surrendered to my Lord, Jesus Christ. Lord forgive me of compromise. I also ask you for courage to approach the pulling down of strongholds without reluctance or willful deception in my heart. By the power of the Holy Spirit and in the Name of Jesus, I bind the satanic influences that were reinforcing compromise and sin within me. I submit myself to the light of the Spirit of Truth to expose the strongholds of sin within me. By the mighty weapons of the Spirit and the Word, I proclaim that each stronghold in my life is coming down! I purpose, by the grace of God, to have only

one stronghold within me: the stronghold of the Presence of Christ!

I thank You, Lord, for forgiving and cleansing me from all my sins. And by the grace of God, I commit myself to follow through in this area until even the ruins of this stronghold are removed from my mind! Thank You, Father. In Jesus' name. Amen.

Reconciliation

- But now we are no more under the curse of the Law of Sin and Death.
- But now we are able to stand.
- But now we are able to run this race with patience, and finish.
- But now we are released from the power of the Prince of Darkness and the Air.
- But now we are able to live lives wholly separated unto God.
- But now our occupation has been changed to that of Sons, who know their Father's voice and no longer follow the voice of the Stranger.

Have you ever been at a point in your life where you were not where you use to be, but you knew you were not where you were going? That is an in between time, a meanwhile time. When the getting there seems to take a long time. This is a time when the redemptive grace of God is being revealed to us. He speaks in the silence of what seems to a place without a name or an explanation. Redemption is bestowed on us from the throne of grace to first repair the estranged relationship between God and ourselves. Out of that restored relationship comes assurance that we are free in Jesus. From that point we are no longer at war with ourselves, but at peace -- because we understand that we are not being punished by God.

We are merely undoing the consequences of all the bad choices we have made so far in life. When we have that peace there is a blessed repose, and the bountiful faith that we are changing as we change our environment.

Our Lives after the Cross

Our ability to stand and have a changed nature was accomplished through the fulfillment of many Old Testament Prophecies, and symbolized through the Last Supper. Isaiah spoke of his coming 750 years plus before his coming. Some Prophets today would be stoned for speaking that prophesy, and it not manifesting by 2 years or less of waiting for his coming.

John 14:30 says 'I'll not be talking with you much more like this because the chief of the godless world is about to attack. But don't worry -- he has nothing on me, no claim on me." (Message Translation, Eugene Peterson)

Remember a vital key is humility. Francis Frangipane, on page 12 in his book "The Three Battlegrounds of the Mind" said, "a vital key to overcoming the devil is humility. To humble yourself is to refuse to defend your image." You are corrupt and full of sin in your old nature! Yet, we have a new nature, which has been created in the likeness of Christ. (Ephesians 4:24). So we can agree with our adversary about the condition of our flesh! The strength of humility is that it builds a spiritual defense around our soul, prohibiting strife, competition and many of life's irritations from stealing our peace.

Galatians 5:21b says, "...of the which I tell you in time past, that they which do such things shall not inherit the kingdom of God."

We are friends and sons. His love flows freely, and he declares in Romans 8:28-39 the following: "And we know that all things work together for the good to them that love God, to them who are the called according to his purpose. For whom he did foreknow, he also did predestinate to be conformed to the image of his Son, that he might be the firstborn among many brethren. Moreover whom he did predestinate, them he also called: and whom he called, them he also justified; and whom he justified them he also glorified. What shall we then say to these things?

If God be for us, who can be against us? He that spared not his own Son, but delivered him up for us all, how shall he not with him also freely give us all things? Who shall lay any thing to the charge of God's elect? It is God that justifieth. Who is he that condemneth? It is Christ that died, yea rather, that is risen again, who is even at the right hand of God, who also maketh intercession for us. Who shall separate us from the love of Christ? Shall tribulation, or distress, or persecution, or famine, or nakedness, or peril, or sword? As it is written, For thy sake we are killed all the daylong: we are accounted as sheep for the slaughter. Nay, in all these things we are more than conquerors through him that loved us. For I am persuaded, that neither death, nor life, nor angels, nor principalities, nor powers, nor things present, nor things to come. Nor height, nor depth, nor any other creature, shall be able to separate us from the love of God, which is in Christ Jesus our Lord."

The veil of the Temple has been torn from the top to the bottom and there is an empty tomb where they laid him! Because He has RISEN as He said He Would! When he arose – you and I arose and for this reason we are now seated in Heavenly places becauses we are now heirs and joint heirs of the promises our Father made to us in the Old Testament! He promised to be our God and we would be his people! No longer turning his back towards us or giving us the silent treatment! He is speaking to us through the volume of His Word, the Holy Bible and clearly thiis book does not contain all, but the summation of the plan of redemption of man back to his creator!

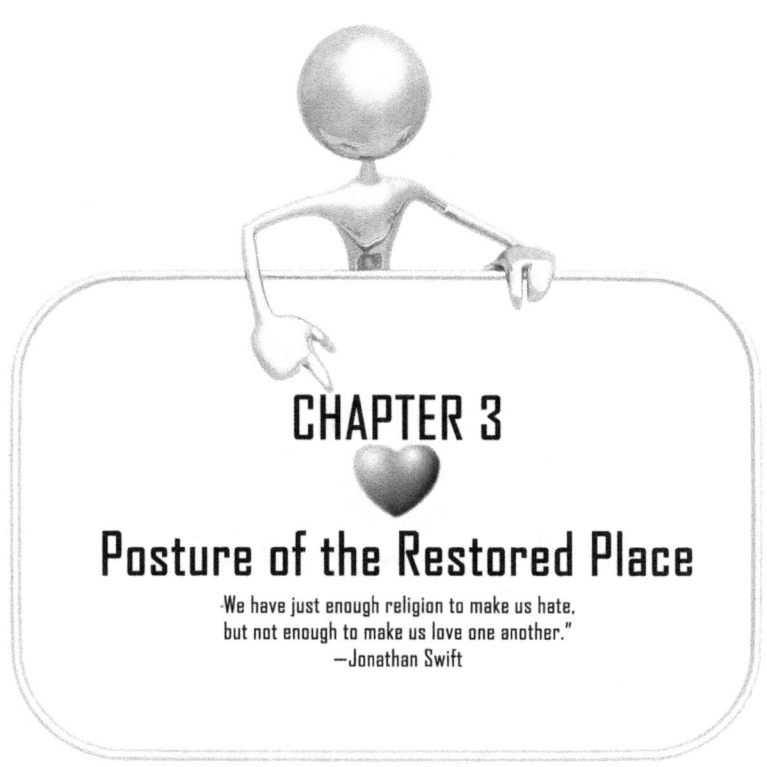

CHAPTER 3

Posture of the Restored Place

"We have just enough religion to make us hate,
but not enough to make us love one another."
—Jonathan Swift

Posture of the Restored Place

3- The Beatitudes (Blessed Behavior)

Your Behavior Is Telling On You

Websters' dictionary says to bless means, "...to invoke divine care for, to speak gratefully of, to confer happiness or prosperity upon. To be blessed means, "...of or enjoying happiness, enjoying the bliss of heaven – used as a title for a beatified (beatify/to make supremely happy, to declare to have attained the blessedness of heaven and authorize the title "Blessed" person) (beatific of possessing, or imparting beatitude, having a blissful or benign appearance)

Jesus said in Matthew 15:3-5, "Now ye are clean through the word, which I have spoken unto you. Abide in me, and I in you. As the branch cannot bear fruit of itself, except it abide in the vine; no more can ye, except ye abide in me. I am the vine, ye are the branches: He that abideth in me, and I in him, the same bringeth forth much fruit: for without me ye can do nothing."

Beatified

Thus the beatified person is not a whining weakling, but a person who has learned the secret of being in a relationship with God.

In Matthew 5:3-12, Jesus said:

- Blessed are the poor in spirit: for theirs is the kingdom of heaven.
- Blessed are they that mourn: for they shall be comforted.
- Blessed are the meek: for they shall inherit the earth.
- Blessed are they which do hunger and thirst after righteousness: for they shall be filled.
- Blessed are the merciful: for they shall see God.
- Blessed are the peacemakers: for they shall be called the children of God.
- Blessed are they which are persecuted for righteousness' sake: for theirs is the kingdom of heaven.
- Blessed are ye, when men shall revile you, and persecute you, and shall say all manner of evil against you falsely, for my sake.

He finished by saying "Rejoice, and be exceeding glad: for great is your reward in heaven: for so persecuted they the prophets which were before you."

Therefore, will all of the beatified people please stand up and rejoice and shout!

The Nine-Fold Fruits of the Spirit

Galatians 5:22

Can be lived out in us daily. As sinners we were some of the hardest work folk on the planet. (Like a famous singer, who won the label as being the hardest working man in show business.) We worked hard at the evil we did in our bodies.

But now Jesus Christ (the Anointed One and His Anointing) tells us to come and learn of him, take his yoke upon us for it is easy, and His burdens are light.

We have only 9 fruits to bear versus the 19 works we were subject to when we were under Satan's control. Satan is the originator of slavery.

But the fruit of the Spirit is...Galatians 5:22-23

1. Love: strong unbreakable devotion to someone. Caring and seeking the highest good for another without motive for personal gain.
2. Joy, delight in your own blessings and others being blessed. Gladness based on the love, grace, blessings, promises, and nearness of God.

3. Peace, quietness, harmony and order in whatever circumstances you are in. Quietness of heart and mind based on the knowledge of our heavenly Father.
4. Longsuffering, without resentment, enduring the failings of others towards you and offenses given and wounding of your heart. Endurance, patience, being slow to anger or despair
5. Gentleness, soft-spoken, virtuous, kind and Godly in lifestyle and conduct. Not wanting to hurt someone or give him or her pain.
6. Goodness, refined as gold in spirit, kind, good, and generous. Zeal for truth and righteousness and a hatred for evil.
7. Faith, divine trust with whole heart in God and all of his Word. Unswerving loyalty to the unity of promise, commitment, and honesty.
8. Meekness, balanced in temper and passions without feeling a need to retaliate. strength and courage, knowing when to be angry and/or submissive
9. Temperance, moderation in all things not given to excessive living or conduct.

Mastering one's own fleshly desires unto purity and chastity.

… against such there is no law."

Paul said in Galatians 5:24-26…

"…they that are Christ's have crucified the flesh with the affections and lusts. If we live in the Spirit, let us walk in the Spirit, Let us not be desirous of vain glory, provoking one another, envying one another."

As…*In Hebrews 11: 32-40, But be…*

'A believer who has and is growing and waxing stronger everyday, no longer making excuses and blaming other people for their behavior and lack. They do not turn back, but allow the fire power of the word to remove the dross (death) out of their spirits and become so full of his presence that the eyes, ears, and heart have an understanding that they are no longer a passageway for Satan and his maggot filled trash in their lives. But able to resist and subdue the kingdom of darkness and stop the mouth of lions...'

Then we can fulfill this fundamental step in being in a relationship with God and proclaiming with the confidence of one who is truly drawn out of the world this passage of scripture that in Ephesians 1:3-14

"Blessed be the God and Father of our Lord Jesus Christ, who hath blessed us with all spiritual blessings in heavenly places in Christ:

According as he hath chosen us in him before the foundation of the world, that we should be holy and without blame before him in love: Having predestinated us unto the adoption of children by Jesus Christ to himself, according to the good pleasure of his will,

To the praise of the glory of his grace, wherein he hath made us accepted in the beloved. In whom we have redemption through his blood, the forgiveness of sins, according to the riches of his grace;

Wherein he hath abounded toward us in all wisdom and prudence; Having made known unto us the mystery of his will, according to his good pleasure which he hath purposed in himself;

That in the dispensation of the fulness of times he might gather together in one all things in Christ, both which are in heaven, and which are on the earth; even in him:

In whom also we have obtained an inheritance, being predestinated according to the purpose of him who worketh all things after the counsel of his own will: That we should be to the praise of his glory, who first trusted in Christ.

In whom ye also trusted, after that ye heard the word of truth, the gospel of your salvation: in whom also after ye believed, ye were sealed with that Holy Spirit of promise,

Which is the earnest of our inheritance until the redemption of the purchased possession, unto the praise of his glory. "

And furthermore in Ephesians 1: 17-22, says "That the God of our Lord Jesus Christ, the Father of the glory, may give unto you the spirit of wisdom and revelation in the knowledge of him:

The eyes of your understanding being enlightened; that ye may know what is the hope of his calling, and what the riches of the glory of his inheritance in the saints,

And what is the exceeding greatness of his power to those (italics mine) who believe, according to the working of his mighty power,

Which he wrought in Christ, when he raised himSELF/JESUS from the dead, and set him at his own right hand in the heavenly places,

Far above all principality, and power, and might, and dominion, and every name that is named, not only in this world, but also in that which is to come:

And hath put all things under his feet, and gave him to be the head over all things to the church; Which is his body, the fullness of him that filleth all in all."

- No longer would his children need someone to point the way to God. But they would hear his voice.
- No longer would He be silent and shut the heavens up for 400 years, completely turn his back on us.
- No longer would we live outside of His presence like dogs and foreigners.
- But we would come boldly before his presence, and be acknowledged by Him as Queen Esther was, and ask what we will from Him.
- He has taken, hewned, carved, and gutted us out like the borrowed tomb for Jesus' burial and greatest war and victory to take place in.
- His grave was hole dug out of the side of a rock, and he was placed inside that rock and became honey in the rock for our natural appetite, living water springing forth from the rock in the wilderness to satisfy our eternal thirst.

We were like the cracked cistern that Jeremiah found himself imprisoned in, where water seeped through and caused the contents of the cistern (dirt/sin) to become unstable mud. Every time Jeremiah tried to stand he would sink, but God had a remedy for that situation.

He sent us a rock that would stabilize and break down the many layers of flinty dirt and sin that that covered our hearts through his son Jesus.

On Christ the Solid Rock We Stand

Before Peter was given the keys to the kingdom in Matthew 16:19, his name was Simon Peter, which meant sinking sand. Afterwards Jesus called him Peter, which meant petra/immoveable rock.

Without our lives being hidden in Christ we are weighted down prey trying to stand up in sinking sand. But with our lives hidden in Christ we are rocks standing on top of rocks, immoveable and always abounding in the work of the Lord.

We are constantly on a course set for completion, with the visible evidence of the race being shown outwardly to our brothers and sisters in Christ and the world.

A life that has been extricated has gone through Deuteronomy 2:1, 3 "Then we turned, and took our journey into the wilderness by the way of the Red sea, as the Lord spake unto me: and we compassed mount Seir many days...Ye have compassed this mountain long enough, turn you northward."

God has no pleasure in our failings, He wants us to succeed (stand) and enter into the promised land.

Secondly, you would have gone through the physical death of the old man. The children of Israel while they were in the problem, had the promises of God on their mind, but not in their hearts. Because of that superficial relationship many of the children of Israel he died in the midst of walking out the promise.

Their emotions were dictated to by external circumstances, and caused them to stumble at the promises of God.

God made them a promise of deliverance from the land of Egypt came 400 years before they were actually delivered. They never stopped believing in the promise while they were in captivity. This is why their cries were heard by the Lord and he sent his servant Moses to bring them out.

Jude 5 says, "I will therefore put you in remembrance, though ye once knew this, how that the Lord, having saved the people out of the land of Egypt, afterward destroyed them that believed not."

Thirdly, we have to walk out the promises of God, and here is where we like the children of Israel falter. The pathway is sure, and the highway is above the jackals that lie in wait to knip at our heels. So what is the problem. Look no further, it is us! We have not learned to stand. We have to go in standing and not crawling, because this land is only for the mature in Christ. When we can stand and enter into our provision (the promises fulfilled of what God has said). Totally trusting that no matter what the external environment appears like, we are on the right path. How many of you have heard that for every level you attain, there is a new level of devil waiting to resist you and cause you to stumble. The word of God is the truth, it is unfaltering and the only compass that points us to the final place of rest. That rest is an assurance and apprehension of heart that since God said, and even though the vision tarries, it shall speak and not lie. Against all odds we are to stand and enter into those provisions. We have got to believe what God has said.

Tommy Cook, said he heard a man say once that, "...there are three harbor lights, which are: 1) the Holy Spirit, 2) the Word of God, and 3) Circumstances. God may speak into your heart something, even confirm it in the Word, and what do we do? But pack our duffel bag and get ready to go right then. God isn't always in it, is He? Circumstances have to work out with the Spirit and with the Word. God will work the circumstances and it will flow in His timing."

Jesus did not escape the problem, he went through the problem and came out victorious. The Bible said we are tempted because of our own lust. There was no lust in Jesus. Jesus was our example. He came through the situation to prove and show you and I how to come through.

Satan quickly pointed out at every turn from Eve to Jesus these religious questions, "Hath God said?...and "If thou be the Son of God...?" So we had better know whose voice we are hearing, and listening to – is it God or Satan!"

God allows problems to test us and purify us in the fire to build us up spiritually. We must not stagger at the promises of Jesus.

"Deuteronony 8:1, "All the commandments which I command thee this day shall ye observe to do, that ye may live, and multiply, and go in and possess the land which the Lord sware unto your fathers. And thou shalt remember all the way which the Lord thy God led thee these forty years in the wilderness, to humble thee, and to prove thee, to know what was in thine heart whether thou wouldest keep his commandments, or no. And he humbled thee, and suffered thee to hunger, and fed thee with manna, which thou knewest not, neither did thy fathers know; that he might make thee know that man doth not live by bread only, but by every word that proceedeth out of the mouth of the Lord doth man live. Thy raiment waxed not old upon thee, neither did thy foot swell, these forty years. Thou shalt also consider in thine heart, that, as a man chasteneth his son, so the Lord thy God chasteneth thee. Therefore thou shalt keep the commandments of the Lord thy God, "to walk in his ways, and to fear him. For the Lord thy God bringeth thee into a good land, a land of brooks of water, of fountains and depths that spring out of valleys and hills; a land of whet, and barley, and vines, and fig trees, and pomegranates; a land of oil olive, and honey; a land wherein thou shalt eat bread without scarceness, thou shalt not lack any thing in it; a land whose stones are iron, and out of whose hills thou mayest dig brass. When thou hast eaten and art full, then thou shalt bless the Lord thy God for the good land which he hath given thee. Beware that thou forget not the Lord thy God, in not keeping his commandments, and his judgments, and his statutes, which I command thee this day. Lest when thou hast eaten and art full, and hast built goodly houses, and dwelt therein; and when thy herds and thy flocks multiply, and thy silver and thy gold is multiplied.

It takes applying pressure to the obstacles in your life with the Word of God to activate the manifestation of the promises of God.

While having the Character of God bore into the very marrow of your bones to maintain the posture of standing while the promise is coming forth.

God has said that we should let nothing separate us from the love of God. Why?

Because it is the moisture that keeps us from drying out and being blown away by the winds of adversity. He the word of God is health to our navels and marrow to our bones. Marrow has to receive the moisture of the blood to continue to do its job in the center of our bones. Without the love of God, we can become bitter, envious, jealous, haters, backbiters, busybodies, and down right inside out ugly. Our bones dry out from sorrow and grief.

Let Your Glory Fill This Place

Numbers 9:15-22a "On the day the Holy Tent, the Tent of the Agreement, was set up, the Lord's cloud covered IT. At night, the cloud over the Holy Tent looked like fire. The cloud stayed over the Holy Tent all the time. And at night the cloud looked like fire. When the cloud moved from its place over the Holy Tent, the Israelites followed it. When the cloud stopped, that is the place where the people of Israel camped. This was the way the Lord showed the people of Israel when to move and when to stop and set up camp. While the cloud stayed over the Holy Tent, the people continued to camp in that same place. Sometimes the cloud would stay over the Holy Tent for a long time. The Israelites obeyed the Lord and did not move. Sometimes the cloud was over the Holy Tent for only a few days. So the people obeyed the Lord's command--they followed the cloud when it moved. Sometime the cloud stayed only during the night-- the next morning the cloud moved. So the people gathered their things and followed it. If the cloud moved, during the day or during the night, then the people followed it. If the cloud stayed over the Holy Tent for two days, or a month, or a year, the people continued to obey the Lord..."

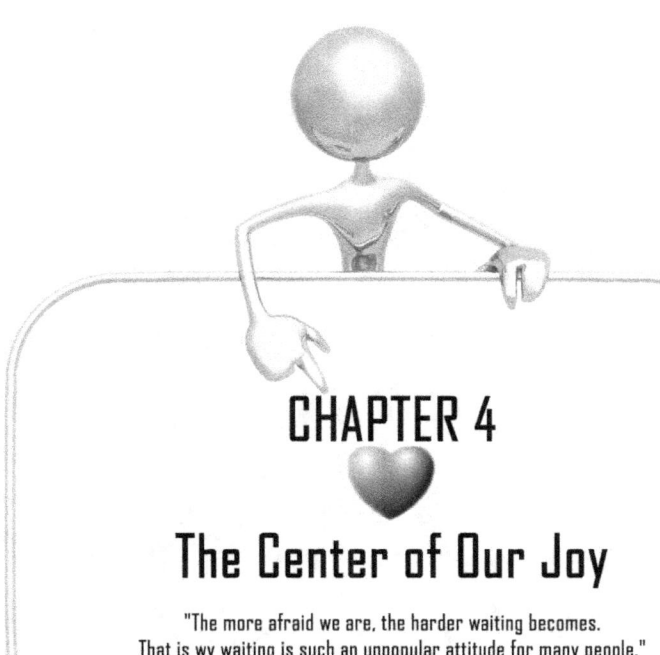

CHAPTER 4

The Center of Our Joy

"The more afraid we are, the harder waiting becomes.
That is wy waiting is such an unpopular attitude for many people."
Henri J.M. Nouwen

The Center of Our Joy

4- Love

The marrow is symbolic of the Joy of the Lord being our strength in our inner man.

The Agape love (Greek) is expressed through available hearts from God. He is love and the demonstration of himself is from breast to breast. As we are commanded to love ye one another. God loved us through Christ by giving us his only begotten son to die for us.

"As I have loved you, so must you love one another" (John 13:34) When were sinners (enemies) of righteousness, he yet loved us. We were unlovely, and so God says by this will all men know that ye are my disciples. Agape is the command of God to every believer as the demonstrated manifestation of our profession of faith.

There is a song that begins like this "Sin demanded JUSTICE for my soul, but MERCY said no...!

I Corinthians 13:4-7 Nkjv

President William McKinley had been pressed upon and attacked by a poor young reporter on numerous occasions. This reporter did not have a winter coat, and he observed him shivering one night outside of his coach. Mr. McKinley stopped and put his overcoat on him and invited him to ride inside of his coach. The reporter replied to his kindness, that he (Mr. McKinley) did not know who he was, I am the one who has been attacking you. Mr. McKinley responded telling the young reporter that he knew who he was, and still proceeded to invite him into the coach and give him his coat. This is a demonstration of blessing those who persecute you at its' finest. How many of us will respond when in a similar situation. Father; help us to be more like you and less like ourselves!

Love is Our Compass! God is Love!

Love Never Fails

I Corinthians 13:8 helps us to understand that a relationship is growth fed. Jesus could do no miracles in their city because they were offended at him. The word of God tells us to be offended in nothing Psalms 119:165.

Romance means to rise or soar. The love of lifts higher than any adversity in our lives. We were created in the image of God for his good pleasure. To pleasure him, and he to pleasure us. The original relationship was one of mutal exchange, both giving completely and totally of one another. Not a 50/50 relationship. He loves us and wants to be loved in return. God so loved us that he gave his only begotten son, and we receive his love when we accept the Gift of his love – Jesus Christ. He loves us not based on who we are, but how he sees his son reflected back at him. When our ways are pleasing to him, he sees us as all together lovely. Deuteronomy 7:7-8. He loved us so much, that he wanted us to dwell with us. In the cool of the day he walked and talked with his creation Adam. God does not want our love under distress or fear of being rejected by him. He does not turn his back on us when we behave unlovely. (Jeremiah 3:14) He indwelt us from the moment we accepted his son into our hearts (I John 4:7,8) John 15:9, tells us how God desires to be loved. Our destiny is hidden in him, rooted and grounded in his love, the viscissitudes of life do not break this relationship, He is no longer seeking to divorce us, as in times past – when we were under the law. Many of us a still behaving like Gomer, a wayward wife who roamed the streets, bringing back to her husband the results of her infidelities. Only to find him still there with open arms, ever forgiving and ever loving. (I Corinthians 13:13)

GRACE the Number 5

Because of the Atonement of Grace through the shed blood of the spotless lamb Jesus, life is received. Christ received 5 wounds in his body that provided access into His presence permanently through the fulfillment of the Law!

Genesis	Ark of Covenant	Mans dominion Satan's dominion Man's will	Headship in heavenly places.	Ephesians 4:11-12. **Apostles** contain the other four
Exodus	Shekinah	God's will overruling. Following the presence of God	Left hand bondage release	**Prophets**
Leviticus	Fire (Sealant)	Sealed until the day of redemption.	Right hand of fellowship	**Evangelist**
Numbers	Urim/Thummim	God left no account of himself or His will.	Feet pointed toward the Earth	**Pastors**
Deuteronomy	400 Silent Years Absent of the prophets. Choice of life or death.	Gods back turned Moses Song of Judgment	Side	**Teachers**

Evangelist — focus on the last but without the responsibility of seeing them through to maturity. Yet without them the church would not remain focused on the unsaved.

Pastors — God-given cautious nature that protects the flock of God. Prevent prophets from going to extremes.

Teachers — are pragmatist by nature enabling them to bring clear direction of the word. But need the cultivation of all the other ministries to prevent forming the word into principles and formulas.

Apostles — are all of these ministries and are given to keep the church on the right path, and labor that God might be formed in His people.

Prophets — are visionaries by nature and prevent stagnation and complacency prophets look for God. So they can point the way.

Luke 14:33 (Perfect heart prevents fragmentation)

Exodus 12:9-10 The whole can not be discerned until the members digest the whole roll. Hebrews 1:1-2 A (God no longer gives clues, he gives the whole) and in Ephesians 4:11-12 and Acts 5:20 (grow up in all aspects) and Psalms 119:160 (sum of thy word is truth).

Mercy

Is God attending to us despite our sins! His loving kindness towards and his tender mercies towards us are not based on how good we have been or shall become. It is his good pleasure to have offered his son for us while we were yet sinners and his enemies! Now that the way of escape has been made for us and the offering has received and found to be acceptable – shall he despise us, reject us and diminish us? No! He loves us even the more that the blood has been shed for us that was pure and clean granting us access to the throne room! What shall we do but come running and obtain mercy in the time of need! Come and obtain mercy for your sorrows! The Ark of the Covenant as a type of the throne of judgment requiring that blood be sprinkled upon it for the sins of the people. No longer is one of judgment but the throne or grace where we obtain mercy! We are able to approach through praise and worship. Merrill F. Unger says that "The ark was the commencement of everything in the Tabernacle…placed in the Holy of Holies, showing that God begins from Himself in His outreach toward man…the human approach the worship begins from without, moving toward God in the very center…Man begins at the bronze altar…at the cross, where atonement is made in the light of the fire of God's judgment."

CHAPTER 5
After Doing All

After Doing All

5- After Doing All

David shouted "You come to me with a sword, a spear, and a javelin, but I come to you in the name of the Lord of Hosts, (El Elyon) the God of the armies of Israel, whom you have taunted. This day the Lord will deliver you up into my hands..." (I Samuel 17:45-46a).

David had sinned many times, but the one thing that caused him to prevail was his heart. He was quick to repent when convicted by God. He would allow God to come into the darkness in his heart and tell him to shine the light and clean up that mess. David knew how to accept God's love and forgiveness, and go on from there and not dwell on the sin he committed once he repented and received God's forgiveness.

We are three fold beings who need and require a three-fold response to our lives.

How do we get to the point of standing? Ephesians 6:10, "Finally my brethren, be strong in the Lord, and in the power of his might."

Your soul must first become persuaded that the necessary strength to stand is not within itself. That the strength needed is found in the power of the Holy Spirit, the Word of God tells us that it is not by power, nor by might, but by his Spirit.

How do you get your soul persuaded? By meditating on the promises in Gods' word, allowing your mind to be renewed. Which means you put on the whole armour of God. Having the ability to stand against, withstand the attacks, and quench the darts of the attacks from Satan. First find out are you your own enemy, by sins un-confessed or reentered into.

If so, confess your sins so that is having your loins girt about with truth. There is no shadow or turning in God, so if there are any shadows or ways that would cause God to turn from you and not to you these need to be washed away. This battle is the Lords, only when we are the righteousness of God through Christ Jesus.

The truth that is to be girt upon your loins is the remission of your sins, that allows every other peace of armour that you put on your body to be supported and stay in it's proper place. You wouldn't want your breastplate to slip down just as an arrow was aimed at your heart. So, having yourself in the righteousness of God through Christ Jesus is the first thing to do when getting dressed.

Then you have legal right to secure the Breastplate of Righteousness to the front of you and the rear of you, and have it extend down to legs. The vital organs are protected with his righteousness, and as the darts are flung at you as a form of accusation against you. God says not so, this is my righteous one and no weapon formed against them shall prosper! It may knock you down, but never out!

Then shod your feet with the preparation of the Gospel of Peace. Meaning that every place that the soles of your feet tread on become marked territory for your victory dance. This covered the front of the legs, and prevented injury from the rocky terrain, and other elements at foot level. No temptation, trial or test can make you stumble at the promises of God. Because a way of escape has already been made.

Above all taking the shield of faith, to defend any area that an attack is being directed towards. Every time you move that shield it is your banner being waved in the face of Satan, that he can not come beyond the place you have marked out with your feet that are shod with the preparation of the Gospel of Peace. With every movement you remind yourself that God is your fortress and you the righteous can run into him and find security. I am not standing alone,

God is contending with those who are contending with me, because I have hidden his word inside of me.

Then the "Helmet of Salvation". Which is the blood covering your soul; that is your mind and emotions being clothed and shielded through the cleansing power of the blood of Jesus. You operate your control tower with the mind of Christ! You are alert to the devices of the enemy, because you are able to hear clearly the instructions from your commanding officer, Jesus Christ!

Then the control tower tells the spirit man that it has come into agreement with the Word of God as the final authority over your life. The Spirit prays to the Father, the word that you have put inside of you through meditation on the word. God is only moved by his own words, and the Spirit knows what the word of God. The Spirit man is not only non-responsive when we are throwing fits, but is grieved that we have not turned inwardly.

Finally, the Sword of the Spirit – which is the unchanging, irrevocable Word of God!

In the battle when you swing the sword, you do so in a back and forth motion, circular motion and up and down motion. You are not only cutting away the snares of Satan, but you are cutting your fleshly will. Meaning that you are in a constant state of surrender and submission to the will of God and the authority of God over your life. It is a double edged sword that divides asunder. It will convict you and confirm you, and remind you to stay in right standing with God. An unrighteous man is a double minded man, who is unstable in all of his ways. Which causes your feet to slip during battle. God said that he would keep the foot of the righteous from slipping and being ensnared. We must endure the call on our lives as good soldiers of faith. Let's examine if after we have done all – if the battle will turn out for our good. Now we must not be getting ready, but BEING READY!!!

Turn to II Samuel, Chapters 7 and 8: David had done all to stand, and he kept his self in the ready mode through this prayer that he offered before the Lord! Be sure to read the full account of chapter 7.

In II Samuel 7:8-9, Now therefore so shalt thou say unto my servant David, Thus saith the Lord of hosts, I took thee from the sheepcote, from following the sheep, to be ruler over my people, over Israel. And I was with thee whithersoever thou wentest, and have cut off all thine enemies out of thy sight, and have made thee a great name, like unto the name of the great men that are in the earth....and continuing in II Samuel 7:18-29

...Then went king David in, and sat before the Lord, and he said, Who am I, O Lord God? And what is my house, that thou hast brought me hitherto? And this was yet a small thing in thy sight, O Lord God; but thou hast spoken also of they servant's house for a great while to come. And is this the manner of man, O Lord God? And what can David say more unto thee? For thou, Lord God, knowest thy servant. For they word's sake, and according to thine own heart, hast thou done all these great things, to make thy servant know them. Wherefore thou art great, O Lord God: for there is none like thee, according to all these great things, to make they servant know them. Wherefore thou are great, O Lord God: for there is none like thee, neither is there any God beside thee, according to all that we have heard with our ears...And now, O Lord God, the word that thou hast spoken concerning his house, establish it for ever, and do as thou hast said. And let thy name be magnified for ever, saying, The Lord of hosts is the God over Israel: and let the house of thy servant, saying, I will build thee an house; therefore hath thy servant found in his heart to pray this prayer unto thee. And now, O Lord God, thou art that God, and thy words be true, and thou hast promised this goodness unto thy servant: Therefore now let it please thee to bless the house of thy servant, that it may continue for ever before thee: for thou, O Lord God, hast spoken it: and with thy blessing let the house of thy servant be blessed for ever.

After David heard from God, and prayed this prayer, look at what God did!

Now let's examine - I Samuel 8:1a, And after this it came to pass, that David smote the Philistines, and subdued them: and David smote the Philistines, and subdued them:

The Dake's Bible gives an account of this battle where sevennations were subdued: (page 338) In the battle were:

- 1,000 chariots with 3 men in each,
- 3,000 horses,
- 700 other horses and riders,
- 20,000 footmen.

If we were to create a makeshift budget this would be the cost of this battle:

- 3,700 horses @ $100 each, comes to $370,000;
- 1,000 chariots @ $200 each, comes to $200,000.
- Sum total of chariots and horses valued at $570,000.
- Men of war killed totaled 63,700.

The Lord God protected David after he repented, and did all to stand! So when David stood he stood not alone, but the Captain of the Host of Heaven!! This is what we are to believe when we have done all to stand!

The word of God works! Yea and Amen!

After the battle was over David set out to gather the goods to build the house of God.

Our giving is part of our acknowledgment to God! The answer is in the tithe and our offerings!

I will repeat, we are three fold beings who need and require a three-fold response to our lives.

We tithe our finances, but we forget to tithe our time and our talents.

Tommy Cook says in the his book "The Three Fold Tithe," This speaks of the outer court or the thirty fold realm, the outer court of the tabernacle represented our (physical) body. fold realm. In this outer court is Passover, the realm of babes...there is another realm which is the sixty fold or Pentecost...most of us are in this state...this is the soul realm, the spiritual tithe...the realm of the mind (the soul) Matthew 23:23, Luke 11:42...notice Jesus did not condemn these people because they paid the natural tithes, but he did condemn them for passing over mercy and faith and the love of God, because that is the weightier matter...it is easy to give out of your pocketbook which is the physical realm…but somebody might need a kind word, or some mercy, or some love, or some justice. (I John 3:16)…because of that we ought to lay down our (soul) life for the brethren. There is a giving of your soul. We must give justice, mercy, love and lay our life down one for another. That is why we should know one another by the spirit and not in this flesh in this hour. The hundred fold realm is (spirit) and the Holy of Holies, tabernacle, sons. ..

This is where God wants us to come to. This is the realm of reality, of fulness…they are that little handful unto God, the holy ones, the pure ones, they are those that have been stripped and purified…they have been stripped totally of the world system and become totally His…this remnant is learning to pas through every purification flame, and shall immerge clean in His sight. There is a tithe that God will return for, first Israel-the outer court, Jerusalem-the Holy Place, Zion-the Holy of Holies."

The church is the Zion remnant, and until he returns we must do all to stand and then stand. Where and how do you give the tithe of the physical, soul and spirit of our time, talent and treasure:

1. where we are fed spiritually
2. with a willing and cheerful heart, Exodus 35:4-5, 21-22,25-26 and 29-30

3. I Corinthians 16:1-2
   a. give on a regular basis
   b. make it personal, not because someone else gave. Matthew 23:23
   c. give as God has prospered you personally, and as you desire to be prospered
4. give according to your ability, freely (Acts 11:29)
5. give cheerfully
6. give with simplicity and generosity (Philippians 4:14-19)
7. give from a pure motive, don't give out of manipulation, or pressure, these types of giving do not get planted in the right soul to produce increase. The soil of your heart is all choked up and in fear, instead of at peace and free. (Acts 20:33)

This applies to giving on the physical of our bodies, our talents, and our finances. You ask why I interjected with this discussion, it is because everything we do, have and desire are drawn out of the tithe. This is what David focused on, he always did what he was supposed to do first, when coming before God. He tithed of his time, talent and treasures. We deal with a God who is relating to us out of his authority, God the Father, God the son, and God the Holy Spirit.

We have to respond to him in threes, we must reconcile ourselves to him through our physical, spiritual and soul.

We command our tripartied being to line up with the headship and authority of the written, spoken and rhema word of God.

Stand

Exodus 14:13, records Moses answer, "Don't be afraid! Don't run away! Just stand still and watch the Lord save you today. You will never see these Egyptians again! And you won't have to do anything but stay calm. The Lord will do the fighting for you." Then the Lord said to Moses, "Why are you still crying to me! Tell the people of Israel to start moving. Raise the walking stick in your hand over the Red Sea, and the sea will split. Then the people can go across on dry land. I have made the Egyptians brave, so they will chase you. But I will show you that I am more powerful than Pharaoh and all of his horses and chariots. Then Egypt will know that I am the Lord. They will honor me when I defeat Pharaoh and his horse soldiers and chariots.

Scripture Reference: Leviticus 26:23, 27, 34 and 37

If you don't learn your lesson after all these those things, and if you still turn against me, then I will also turn against you, I --yes, I (The Lord) -- will punish you seven times for your sins. ..if you still refuse to listen to me, and if you still turn against me, then I will really show my anger! I --yes I (The Lord) -- will punish you seven times for your sins! You will become so hungry that you will eat the bodies of your sons and daughters. I will destroy your high places…" "You will be taken to your enemies country. Your country will be empty. So your land will finally get its rest…the survivors will lose courage in the land of their enemies. They will be scared of everything. They will run around like a leaf being blown by the wind. They will run like someone is chasing them with a sword. They will fall over each other--even when no person is chasing them. You will not be strong enough to stand up against your enemies. ." (Easy to Read Version Bible)

But

Scripture Reference: Leviticus 26:40-46

But maybe the people will confess (admit) their sins. And maybe they will confess the sins of their ancestors. Maybe they will admit that they turned against me….But maybe they will become humble and accept the punishment for their sin…they truly sinned. But if they come to me for help, I will not turn away from them. Why? Because I am the Lord their God! For them, I will remember the

Agreement with their ancestors. I brought their ancestors out of the land of Egypt so I could become their God. The other nations saw those things. I am the Lord! Those are the laws, rules and teachings, that the Lord gave to the people of Israel. Those laws are the Agreement, between the Lord and the people of Israel. The Lord gave those laws to Moses at Mount Sinai and Moses gave them to the people." (Easy to Read Version Bible)

Deuteronomy 7:10-24

"But the Lord punishes people who hate him. He will destroy them. He will not be slow to punish people who hate him. So you must be careful to obey the commands, laws, and rules that I give you today. "If you listen to these laws, and if you are careful to obey them, then the Lord your God will keep his Agreement of love with you. He promised this to your ancestors. He will love you and bless you…You will be blessed more than all the people…And the Lord will take away all your sickness from you. The Lord will not let you catch any of the terrible diseases that you had in Egypt. But the Lord will make your enemies catch these diseases…Don't feel sorry for them. Don't worship their gods! Because they are a trap -- they will ruin your life…Don't be afraid of those people. Why? Because they

Lord your God is with you. He is a great and awesome God. The Lord your God will force those nations to leave your country...the Lord will help you...No man will be able to stop you...their gods...do not want to keep them...or the silver or gold that is on ...it will be like a trap to you it will ruin your life...you must not bring those terrible idols into your homes. You must hate those terrible things! You must destroy those idols!"

Joshua 7:10-15

The Lord said to Joshua, "Why are you down there with your face on the ground? Stand up! The people of Israel sinned against me. They broke the Agreement that I commanded them to obey. They took some of the things that I commanded them to destroy, and they have stolen from me, and they have lied. They have taken those things for themselves. That is why the army of Israel turned and ran away from the fight. They did that because they have done wrong. They should be destroyed. I will not continue to help you. I will not continue to be with you unless you destroy everything I commanded you to destroy. Now go and make the people pure. Tell the people, 'Make yourselves pure. Prepare for tomorrow. The Lord God of Israel says that some people are keeping things that he commanded to be destroyed. You will never be able to defeat your enemies until you throw away those things. "Tomorrow morning you must all stand before the Lord. All of the family groups will stand before the Lord. The Lord will chose one family group. Then only that family group will stand before the Lord. Then the Lord will choose one family group. Then the Lord will choose one clan from that family group. Then that clan must stand before the Lord. Then the Lord will look at each family in that clan. Then the Lord will choose one family. Then the Lord will look at each man in that family. The man who is keeping those things that we should have destroyed will be caught. Then that man will be destroyed by fire. And everything that he owns will be destroyed with him. That man broke the Agreement with the Lord. He has done a very bad thing to the people of Israel!"

Scriptural References for What He Will Do When We Stand!

Psalms 91, Psalms 107, I Samuel 9:27, I Samuel 14:9, I Kings 10:8, I Kings 18:15, Job 33:5, 38:14, Psalms 4:4, Psalms 20:8, Isaiah 8:10, 11:10, 14:24, 28:18, 40:8, Ezekiel 2:1, 13:5, Matthew 12:25, Romans 9:11, 14:4, I Corinthians 16:13, Ephesians 6:14, Phillipians 1:27, Colossians 4:12 and I Thessalonians 2:15.

John W. Ritenbaugh states that "The term "know" implies intimate, experiential knowledge, not merely bookish or theoretical knowledge. He suggests that having an intimate relationship with the Father and Son causes us to become one with them. The only way we can do that is by living the way God does by faith. He walks—lives life—with those who agree with Him. The One who already had this unique relationship with God reveals to us the knowledge of how to do that. Originally given to a spiritually faltering people, Amos 5:4 adds a vital command: "For thus says the LORD to the house of Israel: 'Seek Me and live.'" The word "seek" is not being used in the sense of "search" because God had already revealed Himself to them. Instead, it conveys the sense of "turn to Me," "seek to live as I do," "turn to My way of life," "seek to know Me in intimate detail."

In John 17:3, "eternal" is translated from the Greek aionis. Here, it deals not so much with duration of life, since by itself living forever would not necessarily be good. Rather, it implies "quality." Eternal life is the life of God, the way He lives life. To possess it is to experience a small measure of its splendor now.

Four times in this chapter (verses 6, 11, 12, and 26), Jesus uses the word "name" in reference to God. "Name" represents, identifies, signifies, and encompasses what He is revealing to us about God. It includes what He is in His Person, His attributes, and His purpose. God's name keeps, guards, and sustains us, both by our trusting what it signifies and then, through obedience, expressing what it means. Psalm 9:2, 10 declares, "I will be glad and rejoice in You; I will sing praise to Your name, O Most High. . . . And those who know Your name will put their trust in You; for You, LORD, have not forsaken those who seek You." "Name" does not refer to what He is called or the sound of that name, but to what He is like in His nature and character. We can trust what He is. This has marvelous implications for us. Matthew 28:19-20 says: Go therefore and make disciples of all the nations, baptizing them in the name of the Father and of the Son and of the Holy Spirit, teaching them to observe all things that I have commanded you; and lo, I am with you always, even to the end of the age. The word "in" in verse 19 can just as correctly be translated as "into," meaning that we are immersed into the name of the Father and Son. We now bear that name! They are God, and we are children of God. Baptism and the receipt of the Holy Spirit are the entrance into that name and all it implies! We have entered into the Family of God! Just as a son bears his father's name, God's name is our spiritual family name. Consider for a moment how much God must love Jesus Christ. After all, they have been working together side-by-side for literally countless years—all eternity—in perfect harmony.

Relatively few couples are blessed with outstanding marriages that last fifty years or more. After so long, the depth of their relationship must be close and intimate. If that happens between two human beings in fifty years, what would it be like after a few billion? It would be intimate beyond our comprehension. Such is the depth of God's love for Christ—far beyond our comprehension.

In this verse, Jesus is asking God to reveal two things to the world: that God sent Him and that God loves us as much as He loves Jesus Christ. Understanding the full impact of this verse hinges on a little, two-letter word "as." One definition is "to the same extent or degree; equally." Equally implies no more, no less. This definition makes Jesus' request staggering in its implications! It means we can truthfully say that there is not a being in the universe—including Jesus Christ—whom God loves more than us. Each individual whom God has called can say the same thing. God loves us all at the same incredible, beyond-our comprehension level. This statement also shows Christ's unbelievable love for us. He has been with God forever, yet the Son feels no animosity that our Father loves us just as much, unlike the elder brother in the Parable of the Prodigal Son. In fact, in His prayer Christ is asking God to broadcast this fact to the world! Christ is preeminent in position and responsibility—but not in the Father's love. As the perfect Parent, He does not love any one child more than the others. To underscore this equality of love, notice how other Bible translations handle the word "as." They use words like "even as," "just as," "in the same way," "with the same love as," "as much as," and "just as much as." All emphasize the equality of the Father's love.

On the authority of Jesus Christ, the same Jesus who has been with God forever, we know the Father loves us as much as He loves Jesus—no more, no less. If we consider how much He must love Christ after spending billions of years working together in perfect harmony, that is exactly how much He loves us. The true depth of that love is definitely beyond our comprehension. It takes faith to believe this simple statement of fact."

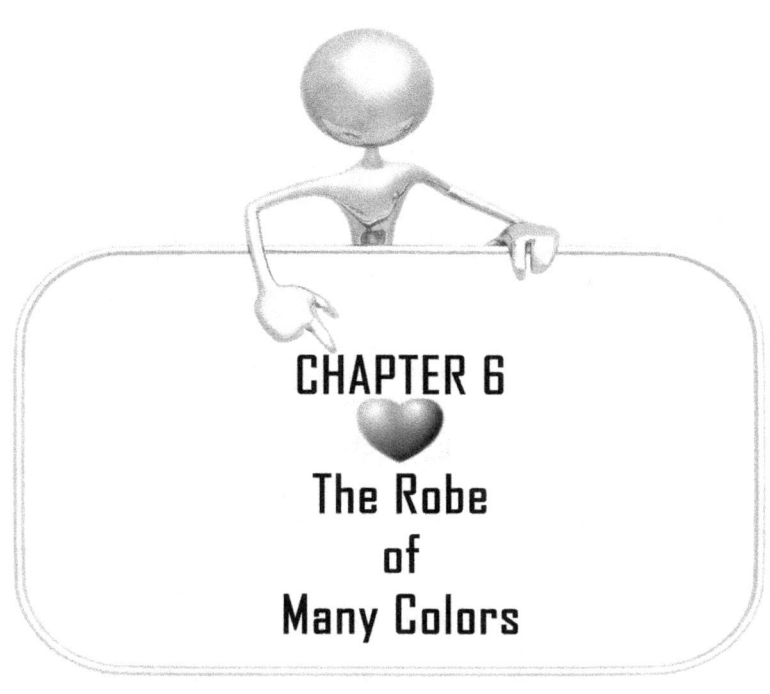

CHAPTER 6
The Robe of Many Colors

The Robe of Many Colors

6 – The Robe of Many Colors

The Relationship (Elohim)

The way the saints are planted is through the storm (whirlwinds). The wind blows seed and pollenates the earth. The Lord our God has made a coat of many colors for his Son, Jesus to wear. (us) The colors are the nations of saints. Like Joseph's father made him a coat of many colors so he has robed us in his righteousness by wearing us next to himself. The breastplate represented the nations of the 12 Tribes of Israel.

Revelation 19:7 "Let us be glad and rejoice, and give honour to him: for the marriage of the Lamb is come, and his WIFE hath MADE herself ready." And in **Matthew 22:1-3**

"And Jesus answered and spake unto them by parables, and said, The kingdom of heaven is like unto a certain king, which made a marraiage for his ons, And he sent forth his servants to call them that were bidden to the wedding, and they would not come."

We have been invited to become spouses, sons, friends and witnesses of Him into all the world! From the foundation of the world he has loved us and planned to redeem us from our bill of divorcement from his presence. Shall we neglect so great a salvation, or shall we accept the invitation and get dressed for the wedding and find him ready to close the door after we arrive to demonstrate how exclusive the invitation to be in his presence is?

Should you choose to accept then surely you will be willing to commit to the relationship in the marriage to the lamb wholeheartedly and allow him to sustain you from faith to faith and glory to glory!

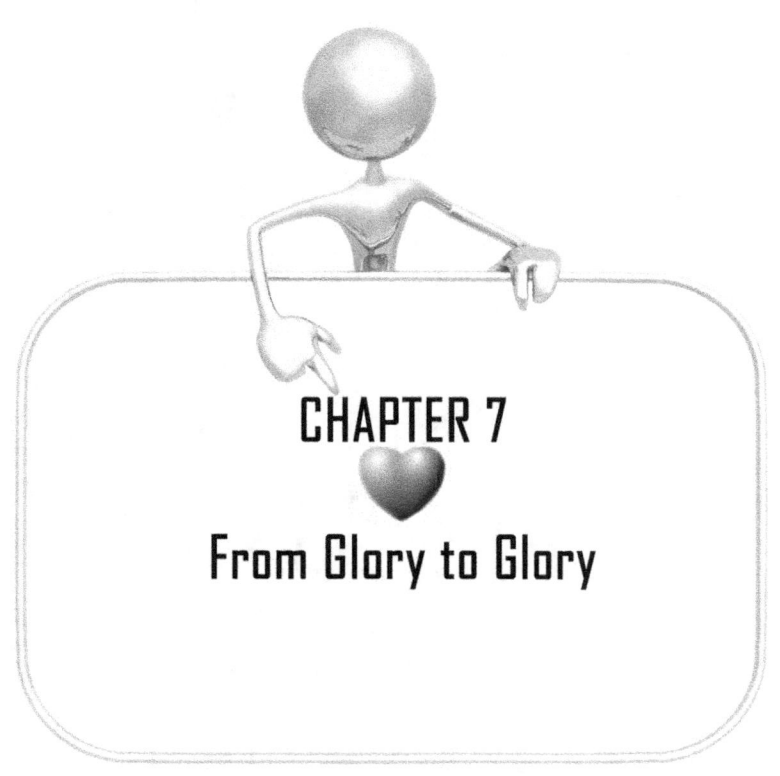

CHAPTER 7

From Glory to Glory

From Glory to Glory

7 – From Glory to Glory

Levels of the Relationship

The Outer Court Relationship

Represents the flesh life, the mouth, and/or the body. The physical house that we live in. Psalms 23:6-8, the evil you consume will be vomitted up in your conversation. Isaiah 26:3, the war in the flesh ceases, and the eye is lit up so the body becomes full of light (Luke 11:34-36. Then Jesus acknowledges and abides in our body as His temple, John 2:19, 21, and John 3:6-7. Habakkuk 2:4, the proud heart....the righteous shall live by faith

As part of the structure of the Outer Court, were the steps and the Porch. The Porch was symbolic of the outward (body) and eyes that which is a foreigner in a strange land to the Holy Spirit. God looks inward, man looks outward and is prideful, afraid, deceptive, carnal, lustful, self-controlled, and indecisive. Yet, he longs to be reunited (but does not know to what). Man misses his first love, and nothing will satisfy but the returning to that first love. Which means you got to stop hanging out on the porch, and come into the house!

Man	Romans 5:12-18
Self-will	Adam vs 12
Selfishness	Cain vs 13
Separation	Murder vs 13
Sensuality	Sodom vs 13
Spiritual Destruction	Gomorrah vs 14
Self-Abasement	Captivity vs 15
Starvation	Self-Denial vs 16-18

There were 7 steps at the entrance of the Outer Court on Solomons Temple, Ezekiel 40:22-34. Seven is God's number of perfection. The scripture tells us that his grace is sufficient for us, and that his strength is made perfect in our weakness. At the outset of seeking God, we need his strength to bridge the gap and enable us to seek after him. The ascent to the Inner Court had 8 steps that led from the Outer Court to the entrance of the Inner Court. The Inner

Court is the place of self-denial and the reconciliation of man to God at the Cross of Calvary. The Brazen Altar and the Laver were the first things the Priest encountered when entering the Inner Court.

The Inner Court Relationship

Represents the souls life that thirst for God. The heart is the window to the soul, and is reflected in the eyes. The mind, reasoning, will and intellect are seated in the heart. God moves on behalf of a perfect heart according to II Chronicles 16:9. The law converts the soul in Psalms 19:7, rejoices the heart in verse 8, keeps the heart pure in verses 9-10, then the heart is acceptable in verses 11-14. In Psalms 86:11-12, he unites our heart (one). Psalms 23:7, the heart is our true self. A divided heart causes spiritual blindness, Matthew 6:21-23, John 12:39-40. Our sight is restored through Romans 8:4-14, and way made to keep our sight. Ephesians 1:18, eye of mind, the heart is the power of perceiving and understanding.

Brazen Altar

The place for atonement. Which symbolized the need for a blood sacrifice, which Jesus became for the remission of mans sins. The Heart, Mind, and the Soul of man acknowledging his lost state, and the need for redemption. It is at this point man reaches out to God and begins to relinquish control of his will to God.

Laver

The place of washing with the water of the word. We acknowledge the hidden sins and desire to be cleansed through and through. It is symbolic of the cleansing power of Jesus, John 13:2-10. The hands and the feet had to be clean on the priest to show they were free from the defilement of sin. The Prince of the Air desires to keep man a slave to sin, but God has made a way of escape through the perfect lamb that was without blemish. Jesus Christ is his name!

The tables outlined are meant to draw parallels that will allow you to see what has been accomplished through the death, burial, resurrection and ascension of our Lord Jesus Christ.

He has satisfied the thirsty soul and made available to us a water that when drinked no man thirst again.

Thirsting of Our Souls

Thirsting of our Soul	Jesus - Romans 5:1-5 (The Ring of Reconciliation)
Turbulence	Peace vs 5
Denied	Access vs 2
Despair	Hope/Joy vs 2
Suffering	Joy vs 3
Perverseness	Righteousness vs 4
Duplicity	Integrity vs 4
Hatred	Love vs 5

The Holy Place

The Curtain drawn between the Inner Court and the Holy Place, was meant to separate by gender and nationality. This curtain was torn which did away with the respecter of person. Satan desires to keep you out of fellowship with God.

The articles in the Holy Place, consisted of the Tables of Shewbread, the Candlestick and the Altar of Incense. The Shewbread taught two truths; Christ is our bread, and the Bible is the bread of life for every believer. The Shewbread was the symbol of the provisions for the voids in our emotions to be filled. The Candlestick represented Christ as the light of the world. Only the Spirit can show us the deep things of God. The Altar of Incense represented our prayers that go up before the throne of God. This is a three fold representation of the Trinity and the path or process one must follow to remain a believer in his pursuit of seeking God. During this pursuit we go from glory to glory and faith to faith See Table below:

State of Reconciliation	Authority Restored Luke 15:11-24
Rejoicing the Heart	Vs 23-24
Reclothed with Righteousness	Vs 22
Reconciled to God	Vs 20
Return to the Garden	Vs 20
Forgiveness	Vs 19
Resolution	Vs 18

Holy of Holies

The Unlimited Presence

Represents the new testament believers full access to abide in the presence of God continually. Luke 10:25-28 Loving God with all of our being. Only He can fulfill the 31,000+ promises because we are one with Him. He will not allow his own to suffer. John 1;1-5, 12-14. At the gate called Beautiful the blind received sight (Jesus, the way, the truth, and the life). In Romans 2:27-29, our hearts are changed as we hear the word and receive it, and are quickened as Christ was quickened.

Hebrews 4:15 all things are laid bare before him. He has given us all power to preach a Gospel that is powerful enough to stand and stop death in our lives. The Body of Christ has received the Jesus on Pilates balcony, the Jesus on the Cross, the Jesus in the Grave. But not the Jesus who went into hell and overthrew Satan, and rolled back the authority of the grave (the stone) and ascended on high and established and restored rightful ownership to the Kingdom of God, over death. I keep saying death, because it is death that has the church in a choke hold. We need to walk in the victory that has been given us to speak to the death in our minds, our homes, our jobs, our finances, our churches and declare that He is Risen from the Dead and He Is Lord!!!! It is a powerless Gospel if we do not preach the authority over the grave! Nothing, and no one can withstand the Lord of Host, who is seated on the right hand of his Father, advocating and interceding and pouring out His spirit into the earth upon the children of God. We are well able to go up and possess the land! See Table Below:

The Veil of the Tabernacle

Separated us from the Holy of Holies from everyone but the High Priest, later torn from top to bottom through Jesus the way into Gods presence.

Ark of the Covenant

Gods' earthly dwelling (spirit) inside were the ten commandments that later become flesh, the Glory of God (Shammah) rested over the Mercy Seat. The testimony, heart and kingdom of God. The hidden treasures, mysteries that are available for revealing his divine presence, blessings, and plans for our lives are shared.

The Ten Commandments

Gods' presence eternally dominating the flesh as original man had dominion over the earth. Oneness, Sanctification, Power, Reconciliation and Inherant Authority. The Lordship of Jesus has given us a birthright that has come from Abraham down to Jesus, and all the names of those between are laided on top of the others and their giftings, callings and anointings are compressed and packed into us through the Holy Spirit. Job 36:11-12, speaks of the life of obedience. The one who lives this life experience the levels of relationship as they grow from faith to faith and glory to glory. Since, there is no fault in God, the fault lies in us. There is no searching of his ways or his knowledge. Pontius Pilate, could find no fault in Him. How can we blame God for where we are not. When things go differently than we plan or expect – we look for someone to blame. Namely God, he blesses us according to our relationship with him. We have no right to blame my Abba (Daddy) because he has done for me what no man could, has or ever will be able to do, love me in spite of myself unconditionally. I say like Pontius Pilate, "I find no fault in him." He is perfect in all of his ways, II Samuel 22:3.

For All Times

Isaiah 53: 1 Who hath believed our report? and to whom is the arm of the LORD revealed? 2 For he shall grow up before him as a tender plant, and as a root out of a dry ground: he hath no form nor comeliness; and when we shall see him, there is no beauty that we should desire him. 3 He is despised and rejected of men; a man of sorrows, and acquainted with grief: and we hid as it were our faces from him; he was despised, and we esteemed him not. 4 Surely he hath borne our griefs, and carried our sorrows: yet we did esteem him stricken, smitten of God, and afflicted. 5 But he was wounded for our transgressions, he was bruised for our iniquities: the chastisement of our peace was upon him; and with his stripes we are healed. 6 All we like sheep have gone astray; we have turned every one to his own way; and the LORD hath laid on him the iniquity of us all. 7 He was oppressed, and he was afflicted, yet he opened not his mouth: he is brought as a lamb to the slaughter, and as a sheep before her shearers is dumb, so he openeth not his mouth. 8 He was taken from prison and from judgment: and who shall declare his generation? for he was cut off out of the land of the living: for the transgression of my people was he stricken. 9 And he made his grave with the wicked, and with the rich in his death; because he had done no violence, neither was any deceit in his mouth. 10 Yet it pleased the LORD to bruise him; he hath put him to grief: when thou shalt make his soul an offering for sin, he shall see his seed, he shall prolong his days, and the pleasure of the LORD shall prosper in his hand. 11 He shall see of the travail of his soul, and shall be satisfied: by his knowledge shall my righteous servant justify many; for he shall bear their iniquities. 12 Therefore will I divide him a portion with the great, and he shall divide the spoil with the strong; because he hath poured out his soul unto death: and he was numbered with the transgressors; and he bare the sin of many, and made intercession for the transgressors.

In the years before our birth, there were many who would be considered ignoble persons who have made it into the lineage of Jesus. Each whose name has a symbolic meaning reflecting the nature of Gods' mercy and love for us. When the Bible says in Isaiah 53 of the iniquities, griefs, sorrows, transgressions, chastisements, peace and judgment was all being reconciled through him from generations before to allow us free access into God's presence. There is a visual of him passing through the annals of time in my mind and picking out the wheat and tare of every ancestral line to be conceived and weaving them into the fabric of his passion. He knew that there would be no other way to wholly perform his Fathers will but to suffer for all of man. Look at some of the names that are included in the lineage of Jesus Christ and their names meanings and see the plan of God to make sure that you and I were not left out of the redemption plan that I have found all point to the sinner we were and the sons we have now become through Jesus Christ.

What Is In the Name of Jesus' Lineage

- Elohim - God of Relationships
- Abram(ham) – exalted father, and father of a multitude
- Ishmael – war
- Isaac – laughter and God will hear
- Jacob – heel catcher, supplanter, he who God protects
- Judah – may he "God" be praised
- Perez – breac
- Zerah – dawning, rising and shining
- Hezron - shut in, blooming or dart of joy
- Aram – exalted
- Amminadab – people of liberality
- Nahshon - enchanting or ominous
- Salmon - peaceable
- Boaz – fleetness (to be nimble)
- Rahab – (broad, wide) in the Greek. Insolence, pride and violence in the Hebrew
- Obed – serving
- Ruth – a female friend
- Jesse - Jehovah exists or firm
- David – beloved or chieftain
- Solomon – peaceable in the Hebrew, also called Jedidiah beloved of Jehovah
- Bathsheba – daughter of the oath
- Rehoboam – enlarger of the people
- Abijah – God is my father or "daddy"
- Asa – healing, to heal, a physician
- Jehosophat –Jehovah judged

- Joram – Jehovah is high
- Uzziah – Jehovah is strength
- Jotham – Jehovah is upright
- Ahaz – possessor
- Hezekiah – Jehovah is strength
- Manasseh – causing to forget
- Amon – faithful
- Josiah – Jehovah heads
- Jehoiachin – Jehovah will establish
- Shealtiel – I have asked God
- Zerubbabel – Seed (progeny)
- Abiud – Father of renown
- Eliakim – God will establish
- Azar – helper
- Ehud - strong or union
- Eleazar – God is helper
- Matthan - a gift
- Jacob - supplanter or followeth after
- Joseph – may he Jehovah add
- Mary – obstinancy, rebellion

He covered all of our personalities and hang-ups and races. Culminating to the point in time where God would no longer go before us as a pillar or over us as a cloud, but in us through the Holy Spirit to comfort us and come along side of us to lead and guide us into all truth. Not even being a member of the Old Testament patriarchy was sufficient to exempt us from the need for redemption. We were forced to rely on the man who would make it through to the Holy of Holies without dying on the way to make atonement for us once a year. This High Priest Jesus Christ did not die on the way to offer the sacrifice for us! He made it to and through the offering up of himself on our behalf for our predecessors and ourselves who dwelt in the outer court. We are to be one as the Father and Jesus are one through the sanctity of the way that has been made for us through the Inner Court relationship.

John 17:17-26 Jesus is praying to the Father, "**Sanctify** them through thy truth: thy word is truth. 18 As thou hast sent me into the world, even so have I also sent them into the world. 19 And for their sakes I sanctify myself, that they also might be sanctified through the truth to **glorify them,** and all other believers with Him in heaven 20 Neither pray I for these alone, but for them also which shall believe on me through their word; 21 That they **all may be one**; as thou, <u>Father, art in me, and I in thee, that they also may be one in</u> us: that the world may believe that thou hast sent me. 22 <u>And the glory which thou gavest me I have given them; that they may be one, even as we are one:</u> 23 I in them, and thou in me, that they may be made perfect in one; and that the world may know that thou hast sent me, and hast loved them, as thou hast loved me. 24 Father, I will that they also, whom thou hast given me, be with me where I am; that they may behold my glory, which thou hast given me: for thou lovedst me before the foundation of the world. 25 Father, the world hath not known thee: but I have known thee, and these have known that thou hast sent me. 26 And I have declared unto them thy name, and will declare it: that the love wherewith thou hast loved me may be in them, and I in them."

Now we all can go from one level to the next as we are inclined to follow and remain in his presence forever. I John 2:1-4, if you love me keep (do) my commandments. He commanded blessings on us and then showed us the way to the blessing. He gave the commandments to the earth to respond when we obey. The earth is the Lord's according to Deuteronomy 28, 29, you will be blessed in the city and in the field, …if we will be willing and obedient we would eat the good of the land.

This state of wellness for you and your household that Jesus fulfilled from the Old Testament and brought it forward into the New Testament: (Leviticus 25:10, 18. Galatians 3:22, Romans 11:36, and Colossians 1:19-20. II Timothy 2:11-13) These words are nchanging, it is a trustworthy statement, that if we are faithless he remains faithful, for he cannot deny himself. Psalms 25:14 the secret of the Lord. He wants us to know Him – be intimately acquainted with his tender loving mercy.

Revelations 1:5-6 and Lamentations 3:37,39 and Matthew 11:6, says our relationship takes us out of the state of living for and by miracles; and moves us into the realm of blessings. The realm of blessings is a place of continual care, and not the state of dependency on the suddenly of miracles. Miracles are needed assistance from God. Blessings are a commanded state of wellness for you and your household.

Reconciling Man to God

Man (Able To Rest)	Jesus (Change of Wills)	God (Restored Authority)
Lying Down Psalms 23:2	Hands= Benevolence Deuteronomy 15:8	Witness Isaiah 43:10
Instructed/Sitting Luke 10:39	Eyes=Vision II Kings 6:17	Salt/Preserved Matthew 5:13
Prepared for War Ephesians 6:14	Ears= Hearing Psalms 40:6	Light/Guide Matthew 5:14
Unity/Fellowship I John 1:7	Lips=Testimony Psalms 51:15	Branches/Fruitful Jeremiah 15:5
Prosper/Running Hebrews 12:1	Spirit=Prayer Daniel 6:10	Doers/Teachers II Corinthians 3:2
Rejoice/Leaping Acts 3:8	Heart=Word Fed Acts 16:14	Ambassadors II Corinthians 5:20
Praise/Soaring Isaiah 40:31	Doors=Servant II Corinthians 2:12	Stewards/Rightly Divide I Peter 4:10

John 3:14-15 tells us clearly, "As Moses lifted up the serpent in the wilderness, even so must the Son of man be lifted up: that whosoever believeth in him should not perish, but have eternal life." To look with the external eyes and believe with the internal eyes of the heart. Faith to believe unto salvation comes by seeing with the eyes of the soul

(external) and comprehending the saving God with the (internal) eyes. Keeping our inward eyes on the Father as Jesus did in Matthew 14:19 "Looking up to heaven, he blessed, and brake, and gave bread to his disciples" when he raised Lazarus from the tomb in John 11:41,"Then they took away the stone from the place where the dead was laid. And Jesus lifted up his eyes, and said, Father, I thank thee that thou hast heard me."

Throughout the ministry of Jesus you find him looking up and this is the way we learn to abide in Him. We look up to block out the external distractions from us. Now you cannot walk always looking up literally, but figuratively your Spirit man that has been empowered desires to do the looking up for you. Keep the Holy Spirit empowered comes from feeding on the Word of God, Prayer, Praise and Worship of God until you are satisfied that when you pray God hears you! There is a time when the quantity time you spend with God becomes the quality time you receive back from God. Quantity precedes quality. Nothing in the bank – nothing out of the bank! Making deposits into your relationship with God before you need Him!

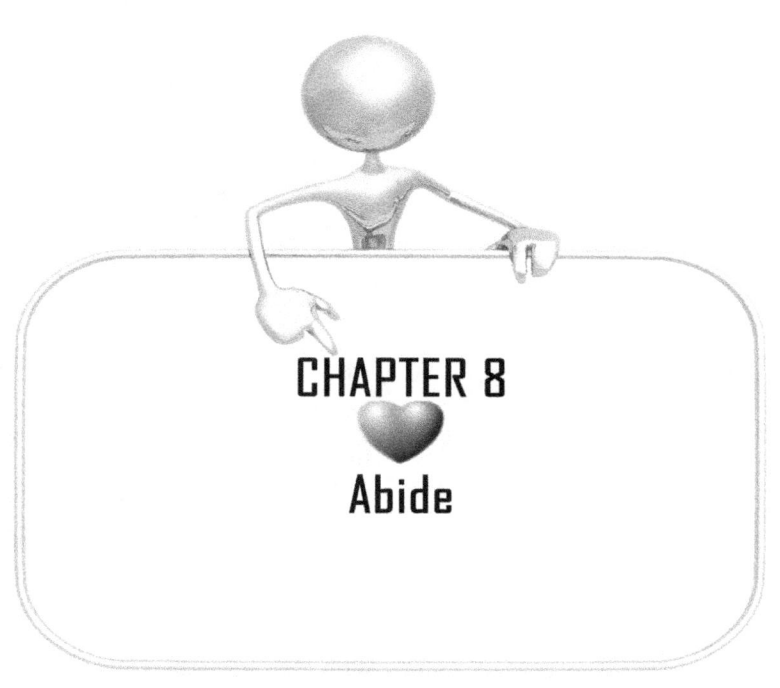

CHAPTER 8
♥
Abide

May the shadow of the wings of the Most High be for ever the dwelling-place' of you all, who **with oneness of heart** *occupy one home? father and mother, bound in the same brotherhood with your sons, being all the children of the one Father. Remember us. " Excerpt from Letter 101 (A.D. 409)*
From Augustine to Memor

Abide

8 – Abide

Through believing on the Lord Jesus Christ and looking unto Jesus the author and finisher of our faith as in Hebrews 12:2 direct the heart to focus on Jesus continuously. Taking your mind from its natural tendency to focus on itself and onto the Lamb of God! We intentionally focus our attention on Jesus, not always being able to maintain that focus due to external distractions for which God already knows about. God takes allowance for that as we grow in grace and does not condemn us for our wavering thoughts as new believers. There does come a time as you are mature in Christ Jesus that you will have formed a habit of focusing on God through Jesus Christ until it has become second nature. The things of the world cannot prevent you from getting into His presence when you sense his desire is to have more of you. This is where you decrease and he increases in your relationship. Your focus moves away from your will and more onto what is required of you from Him. To climb into heaven we must take our focus off of ourselves and how wretched we are and before long the sin conscious soul becomes righteousness conscious and the mind that was in Christ Jesus has now become the mind which rest in you! While you are looking at God through Jesus Christ and gazing at them they are touching you in the secret places of your soul! He reaches inward to us and we must reach outward to Him. We live in this world but we are not of this world, the world requires we focus on the issues of the day, but the heart of your spirit longs to be in Gods' presence. At first opportunity you find yourself rushing back to get into Him. Sounds like a relationship with someone you really want to be with! When you want to be with Him as much as He wants to be with you, seconds away seem like hours! He knows you have to attend to the affairs of this life, but there is a secret place inside of you that senses that you are tied to Him even while you are sitting at your desk, cooking that meal. This is the joy of the Lord because you know without provocation that yours is a special relationship just between the two of you. He is devoted to you and you are devoted to Him! What shall separate you from this love – nothing!

The Fear of the Lord

There is no distance in your relationship and no walls of separation in the divine order of the relationship you have with God! They only exist in your own heart and mind. When Adam and Eve were afraid and fearful of God after the fall it was due to their own consciousness. They were naked before the fall and unashamed before God. After the fall their nakedness become a shameful thing to them, not to God! This is not the fear of the Lord we speak of in this instance. That fear was due to guilt and shame from disobedience. The fear of the Lord is to find yourself on common ground with God about how He sees things. God saw Adam and Eves failure to keep the only commandment He had given them and the penalty for their disobedience would cause a break in their relationship. They were self-aware creatures now and were uncomfortable before their creator. This is the inheritance of the wicked -- that is the fear of godliness. When Adam and Eve fell they hid (became deceptive) which was the result of coming into contact with the deceiver. The result was a trail of broken relationships; with God themselves, broken relationships; with God, themselves, the earth and the things in the earth.

Reverence of God

Disobedience will cause us to lose reverence for God and the things of God. When we reverence God; how does it differ from having the fear of God? When we are deceptive we hide from God and that is what Adam and Eve did. This broken commandment carried a five fold sentence (the curse) of serpent, satan, woman, man and the earth.

God **blessed the Earth**

Genesis 2:74

Genesis 1:28

Genesis 2:5, and

but Cursed Man

Genesis 3:16-19

Genesis 3:14-15

When God makes a request of us and we fail to honor that request for whatever reason; we are irreverent.

Render unto God what is required of God! More than anything else he asks us to follow these guidelines found in Deuteronomy 30:16-20, "In that I command thee this day to love the LORD thy God, to walk in his ways, and to keep his commandments and his statutes and his judgments, that thou mayest live and multiply: and the LORD thy God shall bless thee in the land whither thou goest to possess it. 17 But if thine heart turn away, so that thou wilt not hear, but shalt be drawn away, and worship other gods, and serve them; 18 I denounce unto you this day, that ye shall surely perish, and that ye shall not prolong your days upon the land, whither thou passest over Jordan to go to possess it. 19 I call heaven and earth to record this day against you, that I have set before you life and death, blessing and cursing: therefore choose life, that both thou and thy seed may live: 20 That thou mayest love the LORD thy God, and that thou mayest obey his voice, and that thou mayest cleave unto him: for he is thy life, and the length of thy days: that thou mayest dwell in the land which the LORD sware unto thy fathers, to Abraham, to Isaac, and to Jacob, to give them."

Authority and Fatherhood

Gathering ourselves together in corporate prayer, corporate worship and corporate service are all things God desires of us. Yet, it is the private prayer, private worship and private service to God that aligns us and prepares us for corporate fellowship. God wants you to be so into Him; that should the doors of the church in your community close or your means of transportation fail, or something requiring you to move to a distant place without a local body of believers you will not falter in your faith. You have learned of Him and are able to commune with him wherever you are. Because you know that your relationship is not tied to a physical building but to the True and Living God! Should you find yourself in this place today, here is a prayer for you – "O Lord, I have been tempted to look away from you today, but I chose to look away to you and respond to your call with my whole heart. Cleanse me of all unrighteousness and create in me a clean heart and renew a right spirit within me. Pull the scales off of my eyes that have clouded my eyes that has weakened my ability to see myself as you see me and to see you as you truly are. Wash me and purge me with your blood and keep me with my eyes of my heart fixed upwardly on you, In Jesus Name – Amen.

Sonship and Obedience

Numbers 6:22-27
22 And the LORD spake unto Moses, saying, 23 Speak unto Aaron and unto his sons, saying, On this wise ye shall bless the children of Israel, saying unto them, 24 The LORD bless thee, and keep thee: 25 The LORD make his face shine upon thee, and be gracious unto thee: 26 The LORD lift up his countenance upon thee, and give thee peace. 27 And they shall put my name upon the children of Israel; and I will bless them.
There is an understanding of the Lord as the one Who IS and IS forever and keeps us because he neither slumbers nor sleeps and that his intent over our lives is that we would be one. John declares the unique love of God toward us, in making us His children

I John 3:1-3
Behold, what manner of love the Father hath bestowed upon us, that we should be called the sons of God: therefore the world knoweth us not, because it knew him not. 2 Beloved, now are we the sons of God, and it doth not yet appear what we shall be: but we know that, when he shall appear, we shall be like him; for we shall see him as he is. 3 And every man that hath this hope in him purifieth himself, even as he is pure.

I John 3:10
In this the children of God are manifest, and the children of the devil: whosoever doeth not righteousness is not of God, neither he that loveth not his brother. 11 For this is the message that ye heard from the beginning, that we should love one another. 12 Not as Cain, who was of that wicked one, and slew his brother. And wherefore slew he him? Because his own works were evil, and his brother's righteous. 13 Marvel not, my brethren, if the world hate you. 14 We know that we have passed from death unto life, because we love the brethren. He that loveth not his brother abideth in death. 15 Whosoever hateth his brother is a murderer: and ye know that no murderer hath eternal life abiding in him. 16 Hereby perceive we the love of God, because he laid down his life for us: and we ought to lay down our lives for the brethren. 17 But whoso hath this world's good, and seeth his brother have need, and shutteth up his bowels of compassion from him, how dwelleth the love of God in him? 18 My little children, let us not love in word, neither in tongue; but in deed and in truth. 19 And hereby we know that we are of the truth, and shall assure our hearts before him. 20 For if our heart condemn us, God is greater than our heart, and knoweth all things. 21 Beloved, if our heart condemn us not, then have we confidence toward God. 22 And whatsoever we ask, we receive of him, because we keep his commandments, and do those things that are pleasing in his sight. 23 And this is his commandment, That we should believe on the name of his Son Jesus Christ, and love one another, as he gave us commandment. 24 And he that keepeth his commandments dwelleth in him, and he in him. And hereby we know that he abideth in us, by the Spirit which he hath given us.

In this age of foreclosures and bankruptcy, accept this word from God – that he has taken your soul out of foreclosure and bankruptcy through Jesus Christ!

Disappointments come but all you have to do is stay on the right side of the comma and watch God work it out for you!

God is going to establish the Word of God in your life that you embrace and give you revelation and establish your steps. He wants you to walk in victory through your covenant relationship. This is shaking the dust off or yourself so that God will stand you up at the gate of your soul as High Priest through Jesus Christ, and change you forever toward the kingdom of God. A place of posterity for your generations is what he has had on his mind all alone; according to Jeremiah 29:11.

But we serve a God who will not let us be tempted above that which we can bear! Because He knows the way we take and the frame he has made for us to bear up. His yoke is easy and his burden is light! We have been deceived by Satan and taken on a false-burden onto our frame and a yoke of silver about our necks that weigh us down and beset us. Let us lay aside every weight and sin that doth so easily beset us!

He desires for us to prosper above all things, be in health, even as our soul prospers. Gods' way of bringing us into success is a balanced way of living as he has ordained for us to live! He is not an extremist or out of balance! As his children when we take our journey we are to mark the first

Son of God and walk becoming as Sons of God. From determining that you will serve Him and seek Him "With Oneness of Heart" and "Journey this Road of Oneness Intentionally" so that when you meet up with the "Detours of life that would call you off the Road of Oneness" you are a wise and cunning servant who knows the devices of the enemy that would keep you from an enviable relationship of being able to say that "I and My Father Are One" in purpose! I do what brings honor to God with the ultimate goal in sight of pleasing Him!

Who would dare not to be in the presence of such a relationship? When you see this kind of relationship success in the natural it is to be admired, but to be this relationship! Well that is when the aroma of your praise and your worship come before God as a sweet smelling savor! He no longer smells the stinch of sin of the old man, but the fragrance of a heart that wants more of God with each passing day! What a privilege and an honor to know that he enjoys smelling our relationship! The smell of you excites God! WOW! Imagine You as a the worshipper Kirk Franklin says, "Finally, being Totally Free" from your past and all of the things done to you and by you! Naked and unashamed and smelling good to God!

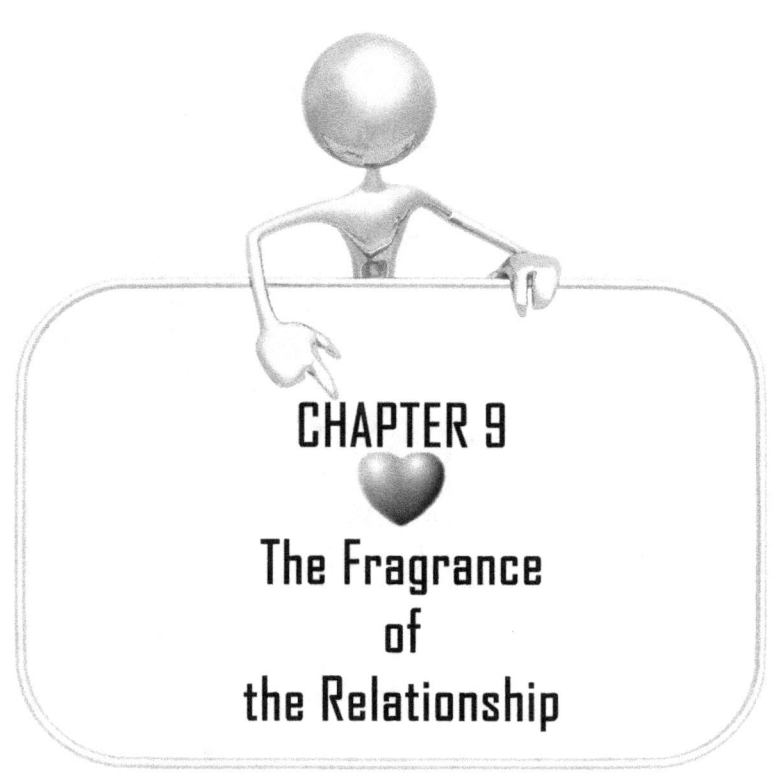

CHAPTER 9

The Fragrance of the Relationship

The Fragrance of the Relationship

9 – The Fragrance of the Relationship

The Root of Bitterness prevents growth. Bitterness carries the seeds of resentment, hatred, unforgiveness, violence, temper, retaliation, murder, jealousy, selfishness, rebellion, and accusation. The fragrance of these things are released as the winds of change blow in our lives. As the rose gives off its' fragrance when fanned so does the tree whose roots are bitterness.

The fragrance of the Root of Jesus promotes growth. The Word says that except a seed fall into the grown and die it abides alone. Jesus was the root of Jesse, and the seed that fell into the earth, the tomb and died a natural death so that the seed of faith could be released when he arose. This relationship is released as our graft is intermingled with the vine. The way the saints of God are planted is through the storms (whirlwinds) that carry the seeds and pollinates the earth. The Lord our God has made a coat of many colors for his son, Jesus to wear. The colors are the nations of people.

Like Josephs' father made him a coat of many colors, so he has with us robed us in his righteousness by wearing us next to himself. The breastplate represented the nations of the twelve tribes of Israel.

The ark is a statement of relationship as God instructed Noah, and he obeyed. When Noah had done all to stand, he stood inside of the ark of safety. Sealed within and sealed without by the pitch between the boards. That pitch was prophetically symbolizing the blood of Jesus that would enclose us in his covenant love. He abides in us as the pitch abides within the planks, and without as we abide within him.

Traditions of man say that the order is God, Country, Family and Job. The Godly order of relationships is God first, and all things are fitted in him. We order our lives in God not around God. All things exist in Him. The Salvation of God (Soteria),

Sozo, safe, delivered, made whole, preserved from danger, loss and destruction, to keep alive. It occurs 54 times in the gospel as to rescue from death of which occurs 14 times. It relates to deliverance from disease or demon possession. 20 times rescue of physical life from peril or instant death. 20 referencing spiritual salvation.

In Psalms 30, we find the answer to Micah 7:8, and Psalms 32. The Song of Solomon is a love affair, which equals our salvation. The lover of our souls. I am today all together lovely, radiant, loved, I am his and he is mine.

Flies in the Ointments Ecclesiastes 10:1

Some types of flies in the ointment of Solomon are doubt, pride and selfishness all which lead us to paths of self-destruction. God is jealous and no other god will he tolerate as interference in your relationship including the relationship with yourself. He desires us to live in the "Zoe" the God life which is found in the kingdom of God relationship of Righteousness, Joy and Peace in the Holy Ghost. A divided heart is the throne room of Satan. It is full of unrighteousness, death, turmoil and the Anti-Christ life that is against God. Self-victimization prevents us from having rest and peace in God. Being in Him is due to our relating with him and not to Him. We can not identify with him as a man does to a man, but must find our identity in Him as we are occupants in him. While we are in Him, he is getting inside of us. After being inside of the unity of the trinity where Father, Son and Holy Spirit are on one accord we come forth persuaded to stand in the God-life.

Pre-Extrication

Extricate means to unravel, to distinguish from a related thing, to free or remove from an entanglement or difficulty. The synonyms for extricate are disentangle, untangle, disencumber, disembarass and to free from what binds or holds back.

A Time of Death and Bondage

Under the curse of the law we were constantly falling, and failing to finish the course before us. We were caught up in the world and its devices, children of Satan who were constantly in a state of disobedience and under his control. The old man fulfilled the works of the flesh because his spirit was governed by the Prince of Darkness. We lived a life devoted to being led by our own passions and lusts. We were sinners by occupation to the sins of lust, divination, false worship and anger.

Sins of Lust

Adultery being unlawful sex between married person other than their mate. Fornication being unlawful sex between persons who are unmarried. Uncleanness being homosexuality, pornography, masturbation, erotica, bestiality, rape, incest, exploitation and raping of children. Lasciviousness being out of control desires and lewd behavior and acting out lewd fantasies.

Sins of Divination and False Worship

Idolatry being worship of statues, picture and images.

Witchcraft conjuring up evil spirits to communicate with and through spells, charms, amulets worn on the body or clothing to ward off or welcome the presence of evil spirits. Inflicting evil upon others through enchantments or to control ones behavior for or against persons.

Sins of Anger

Hatred to the point of bitter dislike, abhorrence, ill thought and hopes on others and holding grudges. Variance creating dissensions, discord, quarreling, debating and disputes. Emulations of jealousy and competition. Wrath that is rage and anger that lingers to the point of creating turmoil and vengeance. Strife filled words with the intent to payback in kind wrongs done to them. Seditions that form cliques, stirring up junk and mess everywhere. Heresies where the truth is not accepted but has its own interpretation. Envyings that promote ill will and jealousy at the good fortune of others. Murders where we seek the destruction of another's life and happiness

Sins of the Stomach

Drunkenness that places you in bondage to alcohol and drugs. Reveling that form riots, obscenities and uninhibited feasting and partying.

All of these are things that the prodigal son experienced in his separation from his fathers house and blessings. Yet, the brother who remained home failed to exercise the benefits provided to him as well.

The Prodigal Son and the Older Brother

The older brother is symbolic of the believer trying to earn the free gift of a life in Jesus Christ. It is free – the gift is yours to take and open and use as often as you desire!

We take the Soul with its inferiority, insecurity, inadequacies, guilt, shame and how we think and feel about ourselves and submit it to the Spirit of God through accepting Salvation that brings with it an assurance of being securely placed in the Kingdom as one who is accepted in the Beloved. He is yours and you are His – a relationship of total commitment. You are a spirit and what is to be desired is that spirit-to-spirt relationship with The Spirit of the Living God! No other relationship has so much to offer you as this relationship does! Intimacy with God comes through Sanctification; which is fellowship and union of spirit until the point that the lesser abdicates the throne in full intention of following the rules of engagement in the relationship with the only wise God our Savior!

Post-extrication

Our ability to stand and have a changed natture was accomplished through the fulfillment of many Old Testament prophecies and symbolized through the Last Supper. Isaiah spoke of his coming 750 years plus before he actually arrived. Some Prophets today would be stoned for speaking that prophesy and it not manifesting by 2 years or less after it had been spoken.

Galatians 5:21b says, "…of the which I tell you in time past, tht they which do such things shall not inherit the kingdom of God."

But now we are no more under the curse of the law of sin and death, but able to stand, and run this race with patience to the finish. We are now released from the power of Satan and able to live lives wholly separated unto God. In

Ephesians the believer is growing and waxing stronger everyday, no longer making excuses and blaming other people for their behavior and lack. They do not turn back, but allow the fire power of the Word of God to remove the dross (death) out of their spirits and become full of the presence of the life God as originally intended. Our eyes, ears and heart have an understanding that they are no longer the passageway for Satan and his maggot filled trash in their lives. The flies are out of the ointment and the fragrance from the apothecary is "Excellence"!

Ephesians Chapter 1:3-14says,

"Blessed be the God and Father of our Lord Jesus Christ, who hath blessed us with all spiritual blessings in heavenly places in Christ: 4 According as he hath chosen us in him before the foundation of the world, that we should be holy and without blame before him in love: 5 Having predestinated us unto the adoption of children by Jesus Christ to himself, according to the good pleasure of his will, 6 To the praise of the glory of his grace, wherein he hath made us accepted in the beloved. 7 In whom we have redemption through his blood, the forgiveness of sins, according to the riches of his grace; 8 Wherein he hath abounded toward us in all wisdom and prudence; 9 Having made known unto us the mystery of his will, according to his good pleasure which he hath purposed in himself: 10 That in the dispensation of the fulness of times he might gather together in one all things in Christ, both which are in heaven, and which are on earth; even in him: 11 In whom also we have obtained an inheritance, being predestinated according to the purpose of him who worketh all things after the counsel of his own will: 12 That we should be to the praise of his glory, who first trusted in Christ. 13 In whom ye also trusted, after that ye heard the word of truth, the gospel of your salvation: in whom also after that ye believed, ye were sealed with that holy Spirit of promise, 14 Which is the earnest of our inheritance until the redemption of the purchased possession, unto the praise of his glory. "

No longer would we need someone to point the way to God, but we would hear his voice and follow. He is no longer silent or has his back turned to us. We no longer live outside the presence of God like dogs, foreigners and scape goats, but we come boldly before his presence as Queen Esther did and ask what we will of Him. We have had the stone of reproach rolled away from us and taken out of the tomb. We have now tasted the honey in the rock and drank of the water springing forth from the rock of our redemption. He has pulled us up out of the cracked cisterns of Jeremiah where water seeped in and caused the dirt to become sinking sand. We could not get our balance and until he became the manifested rock of our salvation. He told Peter that he would build his church "You and I" upon that rock so that the gates of hell would not prevail against us! The keys to the kingdom have been issued and our live are hidden in Christ. We are constant and instant in season and out of season. We run the race with patience and we know whose we are!

In the Care of God

Zechariah 2:1-13 God, in His care for Jerusalem, sends a man to measure it. 1 I lifted up mine eyes again, and looked, and behold a man with a measuring line in his hand. 2 Then said I, Whither goest thou? And he said unto me, To measure Jerusalem, to see what is the breadth thereof, and what is the length thereof. 3 And, behold, the angel that talked with me went forth, and another angel went out to meet him, 4 And said unto him, Run, speak to this young man, saying, Jerusalem shall be inhabited as towns without walls for the multitude of men and cattle therein: 5 For I, saith the LORD, will be unto her a wall of fire round about, and will be the glory in the midst of her. 6 Ho, ho, come forth, and flee from the land of the north, saith the LORD: for I have spread you abroad as the four winds of the heaven, saith the LORD. 7 Deliver thyself, O Zion, that dwellest with the daughter of Babylon. 8 For thus saith the LORD of hosts; After the glory hath he sent me unto the nations which spoiled you: for he that toucheth you toucheth the apple of his eye. 9 For, behold, I will shake mine hand upon them, and they shall be a spoil to their servants: and ye shall know that the LORD of hosts hath sent me. 10 Sing and rejoice, O daughter of Zion: for, lo, I come, and I will dwell in the midst of thee, saith the LORD. 11 And many nations shall be joined to the LORD in that day, and shall be my people: and I will dwell in the midst of thee, and thou shalt know that the LORD of hosts hath sent me unto thee. 12 And the LORD shall inherit Judah his portion in the holy land, and shall choose Jerusalem again. 13 Be silent, O all flesh, before the LORD: for he is raised up out of his holy habitation.

The Zoe

When we are standing in the Trinity we are enclosed and encircled from within and without. Surrounded by their unity the old man in us is squeezed out like the pressing of the olive. The unity of God is entering us and removing the division. As our flesh yields to this process we are changed into His image and likeness from the inside out. We have been redeemed and delivered by Jesus Christ the Messiah! He delivered us from the bondage of sin and death forever. He made us unleavened through His broken body and shed blood as witnessed to in I Corinthians 5:7-8. God kept His promise to us made in Exodus 6:6-7, "Say therefore to the sons of Israel, I am the LORD, and I will bring you out from under the burdens of the Egyptians (sanctification) and I will deliver you from their bondage (judgment) and I will also redeem you with an outstretched arm and with great judgments (redemption) then I will take you for My people and I will be your God (praise). We have been extricated from bondage and into the position of Sons.

Kenneth E. Hagin said, "Get thrilled with the Word of God. Walk in the light of it. Claim what the Word promises and you will reap its benefits. When you become a doer of the Word, not a hearer only, you will become a recipient of all the provisions God made for you in His Word."

Endnotes

MATERIALS
Bibles: King James Version

Books:
Myles Munroe, copyright 1991
Single, Married, Separated & Life After Divorce
Bahamas Faith Ministries Published by Vincom, Inc.
P.O. Box 702400
Tulsa, OK 74170
Reprint Permission Granted by Vincom, Inc.

Eugenia Price
Woman to Woman, copyright 1959
Zondervan Books
Zondervan Publishing House
Grand Rapids, MI 49506
Used by Permission of Zondervan Publishing House

Derek and Ruth Prince
God Is A Matchmaker, 1986
Chosen Books a Division of Baker Book House
P.O. Box 6287
Grand Rapids, MI 49516-6287
Used by Permission of Baker Book House

Spiros Zodhiates
The Complete Word Study – New Testament
Chattanooga, TN 37422
AMG Publishers, 1991
6815 Shallowford Rd.
Box 22000
Reprint Permission Granted by AMG Publishers

Other Volumes in the One Heart Series

VOLUME 1
With Oneness of Heart
ISBN 0-9700976-0-3
Formats: Paper, Audio, E-Book & Digital, Kindle
 Book: Disciple's Guide
Audio: Disciple's Overview

VOLUME 2
Book: Journeying to the Road Called Oneness
ISBN 0-9700976-1-1
Formats: Paper, Audio, E-Book & Digital, Kindle
 Book: Disciple's Guide
Audio: Disciple's Overview

VOLUME 3
Detouring off the Road of Oneness
ISBN 0-9700976-2-X
Formats: Paper, Audio, E-Book & Digital, Kindle
Book: Disciple's Guide
Audio: Disciple's Overview

VOLUME 4
I and My Father Are One
ISBN 0-9700976-3-8
Formats: Paper, Audio, E-Book & Digital, Kindle
 Book: Disciple's Guide
Audio: Disciple's Overview

VOLUME 5
52 Week Devotional & Journal Study/Application
ISBN 09700976-7-0
Formats: Paperback
Website: www.oneheartseries.com
Affiliate Program: www.oneheartseriesaffiliates.com
Radio Network: www.oneheartsoundmedianetwork.com
Email: author@oneheartseries.com

www.ingramcontent.com/pod-product-compliance
Lightning Source LLC
Chambersburg PA
CBHW070337240426
43665CB00045B/2163